AF513743

STRESS-FREE DINNERS

STRESS-FREE DINNERS

Over 90 quick and delicious everyday recipes

Richard Makin

BLOOMSBURY PUBLISHING
LONDON • OXFORD • NEW YORK • NEW DELHI • SYDNEY

For Audrina, Eden,
Jack and Oliver

CONTENTS

Introduction

There are three universal truths of adulthood: fitted sheets never quite fit, the oven clock is permanently wrong and mid-week dinners are a drag. You're already knee-deep in decision fatigue from working, studying or parenting, and suddenly you're expected to whip up something delicious and nourishing - on a Wednesday? Please! Do I look like Martha Stewart?! Add to that the pressure to eat more plants, cook whole foods, and heal your gut microbiome (whatever that means), and it's enough to send anyone reaching for their phone to order a panic kebab, with a side of self-loathing.

But wait, come back! I promise there's a better way. What if you could easily prepare a satisfying, nourishing and genuinely tasty plant-based dinner without the fuss? Game changer, right? That's where I come in. Actually, I've been here the whole time. I found the key under the mat.

I created my food blog, School Night Vegan, nearly ten years ago and in that time, I've gathered a wealth of tips, tricks and hacks that make plant-based cooking quicker, simpler and infinitely more delicious. I've built up my personal dream team of pantry essentials that instantly level up your dinners, and which are easily found in any supermarket. I've perfected flavour shortcuts that deliver maximum impact without maximum effort. And crucially, I've developed a tried-and-tested inner circle of recipes that never let me down when I'm stressed, ravenous and short on time.

My mission with this book is simple: to make mid-week, plant-based cooking feel less overwhelming. I get it - the last thing you want on a busy Wednesday evening is to tackle an intimidating recipe featuring ingredients you've never heard of. You're here to cook dinner, not reinvent the wheel! That's why every recipe in this book is straightforward, streamlined, and uses ingredients you've probably already got in the cupboard.

It's also my guarantee that every recipe in this book is a stand-alone dinner. So when it comes to 7pm and you're cornered by a hoard of hangry pre-schoolers, you won't have to flick past any sides, starters or snacks. Just grab this book and pick a recipe! The entire book is filled with delicious, ready-to-roll, mid-week meals (plus a handful of cheeky desserts) so you kinda can't go wrong. Oops! All bangers! From my Roasted Tomato and Tamarind Dal (page 132) to my Shredded Tofu Enchiladas (page 92), you'll find every recipe nourishing and satisfying, from the first bite to the last.

And finally, I guarantee that these are recipes you'll actually use. They're the recipes I feed to my big family when I go back up North and they're the recipes I stock my freezer with, for easy evenings. They're the recipes I use when I'm too tired to cook and they're the recipes I recommend to friends who want to cook more but don't know where to begin. Just last week, my husband (who is not the cook of the house) made me a bowl of Caramelised Jalapeño Chilli (page 154) from this very book, and I have to say, he absolutely nailed it. Many of these recipes I can practically cook with my eyes closed and it's my hope that, before long, you can too.

I promise you'll be so surprised by what we can whip up with a handful of plant-based ingredients. So, close that delivery app, step away from the take-out menu and grab your apron! With this book, you've got everything you need to become a better plant-based cook - one school night at a time!

A Guide to Stress-Free Cooking

Cooking can be stressful at the best of times, but add to the mix some unfamiliar ingredients, a ticking clock or a chaotic kitchen and you've got yourself a recipe for a pantry panic attack. It's my goal with this book to help transform your cooking experiences into something bordering on gastronomic serenity – like a meditation session, except instead of reaching enlightenment, you'll reach a bowl of pasta. In my years of developing recipes, I've picked up a few tricks that have genuinely changed my kitchen from a zone of mild peril to a place where dinner simply 'comes together' without an existential crisis. (Don't worry, the crisis happens later when my niece asks me what a CD is...) With some simple changes to your kitchen strategy, you'll reach your frying-pan flow state in no time! Cooler than a cucumber salad, fresh from the fridge.

1. BUILD A PANTRY YOU CAN RELY ON

A well-stocked pantry is your mid-week safety net. Keep the basics ready to roll and you'll never be caught off guard. I've put a Pantry Stockers section on page 14, but be sure to keep a personalised list of your most used ingredients. Also, if you have a smart speaker, most have a shopping list function which you can add to each time you run out of an ingredient and can access from your phone. This way, you always have a shopping list to hand and you'll never find yourself without something essential.

2. PREPARATION, PREPARATION, PREPARATION

Before you even look at the stove, get everything chopped, measured and opened. Trust me, nothing raises the heart rate like frantically peeling garlic while your onions are burning. Recipes in this book will list the ingredient alongside any essential prep. So if the ingredients list says 'One onion, finely diced' be sure to do this before starting to cook. Doing your prep up front turns cooking from a sprint into a stroll and helps you keep your cool. I also recommend having what I call a 'bin bowl' to hand, for all your trimmings, peelings and offcuts. This way you're not running to the trash every few seconds.

3. CHOOSE RELIABLE EQUIPMENT

Dull knives and tiny saucepans are the true villains of mid-week cooking. I swear, the vast majority of my kitchen meltdowns have been caused by selecting a pot that's just slightly too small for my needs. Always use a sharp knife and always choose a saucepan or frying pan that's bigger than you think you need. Even swapping a wooden spoon for a silicone spatula can make you feel like you've really got things under control.

4. DIAL DOWN THE HEAT

If you're not searing, charring or summoning the great Balrog of Morgoth, there's rarely any need to crank up the flames. Stick to medium and you'll have time to stir, taste and avoid turning your dinner into charcoal.

5. TIDY AS YOU GO

You don't need a spotless kitchen, you just need to avoid sink Jenga. Rinse a bowl here, wipe a surface there and if you know you're done with a particular thing, tuck it away in the dishwasher. When chaos doesn't pile up around you, stress magically shrinks.

6. COOK FOR FUTURE YOU

Future You is tired, hungry and probably scrolling desperately for dinner ideas. Present You can fix that. If you're time-rich, double your sauce or chop extra veg and pop it in the freezer. It's the culinary equivalent of leaving a £20 note in last year's coat pocket.

7. PACE YOURSELF

If you find yourself with only 5 minutes before you need to leave the house, don't start a 30-minute recipe! You'd think this goes without saying, but one of the biggest sources of kitchen stress is time. Pick a recipe that you know you have time for, to reduce the tension. To help you decide, I've included estimated cook times for all recipes in this book, ranging from 5 minutes to 25 minutes. Oh and if you're already hangry, head to the Super-Quick Suppers (page 113) or the No-Cook Nights (page 191) chapters for quick, effortless dinners!

How to Use This Book

This book works slightly differently from most cookbooks, so let me show you how to get the most out of it.

Like all good cook books, you'll want to start at the end. That's where you'll find a special collection of quick homemade condiments called 'Dinner Dial-Ups' (page 239). These simple but flavour-packed recipes are designed to instantly upgrade any meal, whether you're cooking from this book or sticking to an old favourite. Dial up your ramen with my Crispy Garlic Chilli Oil (page 245), or give your tacos a tasty boost with my Cheat's Salsa Macha (page 247). They're all fridge- or shelf-stable, meaning you can make them once and enjoy them multiple times. Plus, I've included handy suggestions at the end of relevant recipes throughout the book, showing exactly where these Dinner Dial-Ups can shine.

Since this book focuses almost entirely on dinners, I've structured the chapters around the kind of weeknight you might be having, rather than by meal type or course. Need a speedy, satisfying dinner just for you? Flip straight to Dining Solo (page 21) and get cooking! Perhaps tomorrow you're feeding the entire family and still want some downtime before bath and bedtime stories? The Family Feasts chapter (page 145) has got you covered. There's also Super-Quick Suppers (page 113), filled with recipes you can make in under 25 minutes, Make-Ahead Meals (page 55) for those who love to prep in advance, and No-Cook Nights (page 191) for evenings when turning on the stove feels like a stretch too far.

And let's not forget dessert! In Fast 'n' Sweet (page 213), you'll find a selection of quick, easy and delicious plant-based desserts that are perfect for rounding off any mid-week meal.

To help you plan efficiently, I've included the prep time and cook time at the top of every recipe, making it easy to choose a dish that fits your schedule. Oh, and a quick tip from me: measure and prep all your ingredients according to the ingredients list before you start cooking - it streamlines the process and helps to avoid mistakes down the line.

Finally, don't feel bound by the ingredients I've suggested. If you're not a fan of tempeh but love the sound of my Tempeh Tikka Masala (page 89), feel free to swap it for tofu, chickpeas or even your favourite store-bought vegan protein alternative. This book isn't about achieving culinary perfection -it's about creating practical, delicious mid-week dinners you'll actually want to cook and eat. Adapt the recipes however you like; whatever it takes to get a delicious vegan dinner on the table!

Ingredients

From the outset, I decided this book was going to be different, starting with the ingredients. I set myself one clear rule: every ingredient must be easily available at my local supermarket. While lots of cookbooks (including my first one!) call for weird and wonderful ingredients, this time I wanted to make life simpler. Sure, exotic ingredients can be fun, but let's face it - most nights, you just want dinner on the table without the fuss.

So, for this book, I've challenged myself to rely exclusively on ingredients you can easily pick up during your weekly shop. The excitement here isn't about tracking down rare ingredients; it's about transforming familiar supermarket staples into something extraordinary. My hope is that you'll find creativity and joy in how these everyday ingredients come together in new, delicious ways.

To help you stay prepared, I've included my 'Pantry Stockers' overleaf, which is a list of the most commonly used ingredients throughout this book. These are all super-useful, multi-purpose ingredients (whether you're cooking from this book or not), so take a quick snap of this list with your phone for easy reference when you're in the supermarket.

I've also made sure that if an ingredient is slightly less common, you'll find multiple recipes to use it in. No more buying something unusual, using it once, and then losing it forever to 'back-of-the-fridge' purgatory. Every ingredient earns its spot on your shelf. And wherever possible, I've given a more-common-ingredient substitution too, to save you from a wild goose chase around the shops. Oh and the 'Use It Again' table (pages 16-17) will help you quickly find which other recipes make use of that specialist ingredient.

PANTRY STOCKERS

Vegan food has a bad reputation for using weird ingredients that nobody has heard of. Want a lasagna? You'll need half a teaspoon of early-harvest, biodynamic chrysanthemum starch from the foothills of Mount Fuji. Even I've been guilty of getting a bit mad scientist with my ingredients, but not this time! This book keeps things simple, so all ingredients should be super familiar and easy to find in your local supermarket. To help you prepare for kitchen success, I've made a list of the most-used ingredients in this book, so you know who the main characters are before even getting started. Take a picture of this page with your phone to make sure you never find yourself wandering aimlessly around the teabag aisle like someone's lost kid.

STAPLES & SAUCES

Tomato purée
Miso paste
Olive oil
White wine vinegar
Balsamic vinegar
Maple syrup or brown sugar
Nutritional yeast
Gochujang paste
Chipotle paste
Dijon mustard
Sriracha
Soy sauce
Vegan Worcestershire sauce (I use Henderson's Relish or Mushroom Ketchup)
Canned tomatoes
Canned coconut milk
Passata

PROTEINS

Silken tofu
Medium tofu
Extra-firm tofu
Tempeh
Smoked tempeh
Canned butter beans
Canned black beans
Canned cannellini beans
Canned chickpeas
Canned lentils

DAIRY ALTERNATIVES

Plant milk
Vegan cream cheese
Vegan feta
Vegan vanilla ice cream
Vegan yoghurt

DRY HERBS & SPICES

Garlic powder
Onion powder
Smoked paprika
Ground cumin
Ground coriander
Chilli flakes
Dried thyme
Dried oregano

FRESH VEGETABLES

Shallots and onions
Garlic
Mushrooms
Red peppers
Cauliflower
Green beans
Spinach and kale
Tomatoes (vine, cherry)
Fresh basil
Fresh chives
Fresh coriander
Fresh dill
Fresh parsley

CARBS & GRAINS

Jasmine rice
Basmati rice
Brown basmati rice
Quinoa
Couscous
Microwaveable grains
Dried pasta
Filo pastry
Shortcrust pastry
Puff pastry
Sliced sourdough
Flatbreads
Frozen parathas

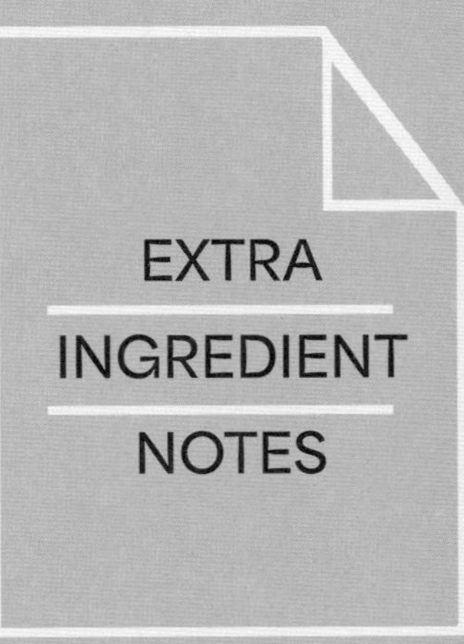

EXTRA INGREDIENT NOTES

Tofu - Remember, there are many different types and they're all different, so try to use the one specified in the ingredients list. Silken tofu is the super-soft stuff that tends to come in a shelf-stable carton. Medium tofu is spongy and comes water-packed in a plastic tray. Extra-firm tofu tends to be vacuum packed and has been pre-pressed to a much meatier texture. I use Clearspring, Cauldron and Tofoo, respectively.

Plant milk and vegan yoghurt - These appear throughout the book and serve multiple purposes. I always recommend using soy milk or oat milk, as they have the mildest flavours, but you should always use an unflavoured and unsweetened variety. I use Alpro Organic Soy Milk No Sugars or Oatly Barista respectively. The same applies to yoghurt; always use unflavoured and unsweetened. I use Coconut Collaborative plain unsweetened.

Vegan cheeses - I've tried to use these as little as possible throughout the book, but you'll find vegan feta and vegan cream cheese here and there. I use Violife for both.

Bread, flatbreads and parathas - I try to keep my freezer stocked with some combination of these, because they can make or break a dinner. Some flatbreads contain milk or eggs and some parathas are made with butter or ghee, so be sure to read the ingredients before buying. Oh, and be sure to slice bread (if it isn't already) before freezing.

Store-bought pastry - Most store-bought pastry in the UK is vegan. The non-vegan ones usually declare themselves as 'all-butter' varieties, but it's still smart to read the ingredients just to be sure. I use the pre-rolled packs for convenience and usually have one frozen for emergencies.

Rice and Grains - Mostly I recommend cooking these from scratch (see my cheat sheet on pages 18-19), but occasionally in this book I'll use microwave pouches for convenience, particularly in no-cook recipes. Feel free to sub these out though, with freshly cooked or leftover rice or grains instead.

USE IT AGAIN!

Remember when you bought a jar of tamarind paste because that recipe said it was essential and now, two years later, you still have a near-full jar lurking in your fridge door? Yeah, same. But don't worry. I'm willing to bet you already own most of the ingredients used in this cookbook, and for anything you do need to buy, I've made sure it appears multiple times so you're never left with an unexpected fridge squatter. Also, below is a list of specialist ingredients alongside the recipes they appear in, just in case you want to plan meals around using them up.

CANNED JACKFRUIT

Instant Pot Jackfruit Rendang (page 111)

BBQ Jackfruit Sliders with Ranch Slaw (page 158)

CHINESE BLACK VINEGAR

Quick Kimchi Biang Biang Noodles (page 129)

Kimchi Pancake (page 22)

SUSHI GINGER

Sick Day Soba Ramen (page 46)

Pink Poke Bowl (page 197)

DRIED MUSHROOMS

Ultimate Umami Paste (page 243)

Balsamic Mushroom Ragu (page 97)

GINGER PASTE

Quick Curry Udon for One (page 41)

Muffin Tin Samosas (Quick Coriander Chutney) (page 106)

Instant Pot Jackfruit Rendang (page 111)

Red Curry Fishless Cakes with Peanut Slaw (page 78)

Kitchen Sink Fried Rice (page 117)

Sticky Mango Tofu (page 121)

Quick Kimchi Biang Biang Noodles (page 129)

Roasted Tomato and Tamarind Dal (page 132)

Spring Veg Yaki Udon (page 124)

Microwave Ginger and Maple Syrup Pudding (page 217)

GOCHUJANG

Miso Butter Cabbage with Gochujang White Beans (page 25)

Kitchen Sink Fried Rice (page 117)

One-Pot Gochujang Pasta with Chive Oil (page 139)

Speedy Satay Silken Tofu with Smacked Cucumber Salad (page 194)

Spicy Tahini Lime Noodles (page 201)

Gochujang Crabless Rolls (page 205)

NORI SHEETS

Ultimate Umami Paste (page 243)

Pink Poke Bowl (page 197)

Spicy Beet and Mango Rice Paper Tostadas (page 198)

GRAM FLOUR

Mushroom Tikka Kebabs with Lime Pickle Yoghurt (page 56)

Leftover Pasta Frittata (page 161)

MARMITE

Ultimate Umami Paste (page 243)

Balsamic Mushroom Ragu (page 97)

Smoky Squash Spaghetti (page 102)

Bonfire Pasties (page 63)

CHIPOTLE PASTE

Cheat's Salsa Macha (page 247)

Spicy Corn and Tomato Soup (page 45)

Shredded Tofu Enchiladas (page 92)

Tray Bake Tofu Tinga Tacos (page 171)

MISO PASTE

Ultimate Umami Paste (page 243)

Tofu Crème Fraîche (page 241)

Miso Butter Cabbage with Gochujang White Beans (page 25)

Stout and Mustard Rarebit with Apple Slaw (page 42)

Spicy Corn and Tomato Soup (page 45)

Smoky Sobrasada Gnocchi (page 51)

Roasted Cauliflower Soup (page 75)

Roasted Shallot and Kimchi Macaroni (page 181)

Roasted Carrot Pasta (page 175)

Cheese and Chive Scones with Mushroom Gravy (page 187)

Baked Miso Mushroom Rice (page 176)

Ultra-Fudgy Instant Miso Brownie (page 229)

TAMARIND PASTE

Instant Pot Jackfruit Rendang (page 111)

Roasted Tomato and Tamarind Dal (page 132)

Spicy Mango Tamarind Sorbet (page 216)

VEGAN WORCESTERSHIRE SAUCE

Balsamic Mushroom Ragu (page 97)

Stout and Mustard Rarebit with Apple Slaw (page 42)

Mushroom Quinoa Burgers (page 81)

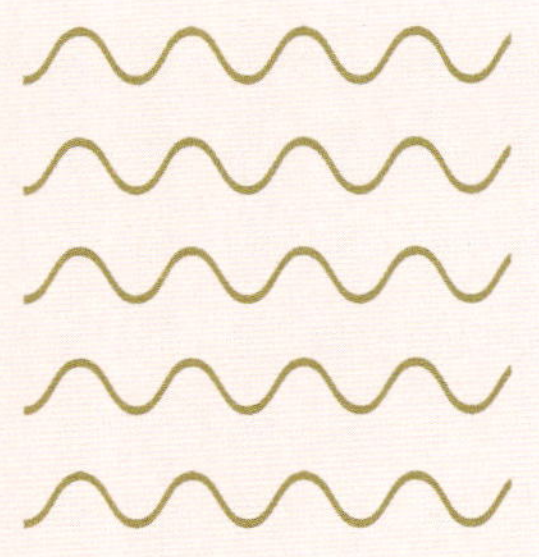

Quick Kitchen Cheat Sheet

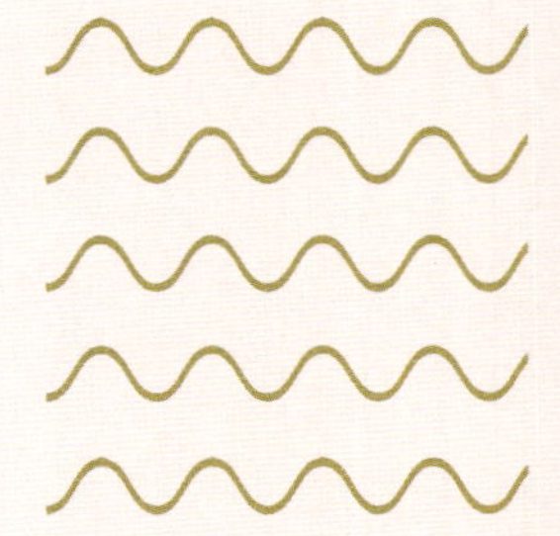

If you're anything like me, you can memorise every line from *Romy and Michele's High School Reunion*, but somehow can't retain a simple ratio for cooking rice. Fear not! I've saved you from perpetually Googling 'How do I cook rice again?' as well as a bunch of other frantic kitchen searches with this Quick Kitchen Cheat Sheet.

For the grains, I've used ratios, so you can easily scale up or down to match your recipe, but keep in mind that the ratio refers to volume, so one cup of basmati rice will require two cups of water.

The dressings listed are each enough for a generous two-person salad.

And for the veggies, these are rough estimates which will vary depending on how you slice them (literally), so use this table as a guide but be sure to check done-ness with a fork before serving.

No more panics, just perfect grains, dressings and veggies every time!

GRAINS	Wash and drain through sieve	Grain to water ratio	Cover with cold water	Cover with boiling water	Bring to simmer and remove from heat after	Leave covered for
Jasmine, long grain and basmati rice	Yes	1:2	Yes	No	15 minutes	10 minutes
Brown long grain and brown basmati rice	Yes	1:1.25	Yes	No	30 minutes	10 minutes
Quinoa	Yes	1:2	Yes	No	15 minutes	5 minutes
Couscous	No	1:1	No	Yes (or boiling stock)	N/A	10 minutes
Coarse bulgur wheat	Yes	1:1.5	Yes (or stock)	No	10 minutes	10 minutes

DRESSINGS	French		Balsamic		Peanut and Lime		Mediterranean	
Oil	extra-virgin olive	3 tbsp	extra-virgin olive	3 tbsp	toasted sesame	1 tbsp	extra-virgin olive	1 tbsp
Acid	white wine vinegar	1 tbsp	balsamic vinegar	1½ tbsp	lime juice	2 tbsp	lemon juice	2 tbsp
Sweetness	maple or agave syrup	1 tsp	maple or agave syrup	½ tsp	brown sugar	1 tsp	maple or agave syrup	1 tsp
Emulsifier	Dijon mustard	1 tsp	Dijon mustard	1 tsp	peanut butter	2 tbsp	vegan yoghurt	2 tbsp
Minced garlic		1 clove		1 clove		1 clove		2 cloves
Seasoning	salt and pepper	¼ tsp each	salt and pepper	¼ tsp each	salt	pinch	salt and pepper	¼ tsp each
Extras					sriracha	1 tsp	dried oregano	¼ tsp

VEGETABLE	Boiling time	Steaming time	Roasting time	Roasting temperature (°C)
Broccoli (florets)	4-6 minutes	5-7 minutes	15-20 minutes	200°C
Carrots (sliced into coins)	6-8 minutes	8-10 minutes	15-20 minutes	200°C
Cauliflower (florets)	4-6 minutes	5-7 minutes	20-25 minutes	200°C
Edamame beans	3-4 minutes	5-7 minutes	12-15 minutes	200°C
Garden peas	2-3 minutes	3-4 minutes	Not recommended	-
Green beans	4-5 minutes	5-7 minutes	12-15 minutes	200°C
Kale	4-5 minutes	5-7 minutes	10-12 minutes	180°C
New potatoes (halved)	10-12 minutes	15-20 minutes	25-35 minutes	200°C

Dining Solo

This chapter, as you can probably imagine, is all about you, yourself and you. I'm imagining you've been out of the house all day - maybe at work, maybe at school, maybe planning a charity bake sale for your local branch of the Hell's Angels. Either way, you've been busy, with no autonomy over what you eat, when you eat it or *how* you eat it. But now you're home, by yourself, and hungrier than you can remember being in a long while. You need a single portion of something mind-blowing and you need it like ten minutes ago. Well, you flipped to the right page, pal!

Every recipe in this chapter is specifically designed to serve one person, without compromising on flavour. They're also super easy and quick to make, so you won't be wasting your precious alone time in the kitchen. Try my Spicy Corn and Tomato Soup (page 45) for a 20-minute supper that can be made with fresh, canned or frozen corn. Or how about a bowl of Bombay Butter Beans (page 30), packed with fibre and plant-based protein, and made almost entirely from store-cupboard ingredients. If you're cooking for one but don't want to miss out on the fun, I've got you covered.

Serves 1

Prep time:
5 minutes

Cooking time:
14 minutes

Kimchi Pancake with Pickled Carrot

For the pancake
60g plain flour
40g cornflour
½ tsp baking powder
¼ tsp salt
2 tsp gochugaru chilli flakes (or any mild chilli flakes)
70g vegan kimchi
2 spring onions, chopped into 2.5cm lengths
1 tbsp vegetable oil

For the pickled carrot
60g carrot, julienned
3 tbsp rice vinegar (or any white vinegar)
Pinch of fine sea salt

For serving (all optional)
Sesame seeds
Sriracha
Chinese black vinegar (or balsamic vinegar)

When I've got half an hour to make and eat dinner, this is what I cook. Yes, I know, you shouldn't eat that quickly, but sometimes you're late for salsa class, or whatever! The ingredients are mostly from the store cupboard and it's so satisfyingly easy to whip up. The pancake itself is chewy and filling, with the fresh tang of kimchi. Be sure to dunk it in Chinese black vinegar if you have any, or balsamic if you don't.

1 Start by making the pickled carrot by combining the julienned carrot with the vinegar and salt in a bowl. Set aside.

2 In a mixing bowl, combine the flour, cornflour, baking powder, salt and gochugaru.

3 Squeeze the vegan kimchi over a bowl to collect the juices, then set the kimchi aside. You should get around 30-40ml kimchi juice. Add 100ml cold water to the reserved juice.

4 Pour the kimchi juice mixture into the dry ingredients and whisk until smooth. Fold in the kimchi and chopped spring onions.

5 Heat the vegetable oil in a non-stick frying pan over medium heat. Pour in the batter, spreading it evenly. Fry for 5-7 minutes on each side until golden and crisp.

6 Once the pancake is cooked, transfer it to a board and slice into six pieces. Drain the carrots and place on top of the pancake, then sprinkle with sesame seeds. Drizzle with sriracha and dunk in Chinese black vinegar (or balsamic if you don't have any), if you like.

Serves 1

Prep time: 5 minutes

Cooking time: 25 minutes

Miso Butter Cabbage with Gochujang White Beans

½ sweetheart cabbage (halve it lengthways)
40g vegan butter, at room temperature
1 tbsp miso paste
1 large garlic clove, minced
1 x 400g can cannellini beans
1 tbsp gochujang
1 vegetable stock cube

When you've got the house to yourself, sometimes you just need to eat half a cabbage for dinner, and I can't think of a better way to do it than this. Be brave when charring the cabbage in the dry frying pan; you want a decent amount of colour to amp up the flavour dramatically. Oh, and there's no need to drain your can of beans! Baking them in that thick starchy soaking water will help them to stay glossy and super flavoursome.

1 Preheat the oven to 220°C/Fan 200°C/Gas Mark 7.

2 Heat a cast-iron skillet or ovenproof frying pan over high heat. Place the cabbage in the hot pan, cut-side down, and sear until charred – around 3–4 minutes.

3 In a small bowl, mix together the vegan butter, miso paste and minced garlic.

4 Remove the cabbage from the pan and set aside. Add the entire can of cannellini beans, including the soaking water, to the skillet. Fill the can halfway with water and pour it into the skillet. Add the gochujang and stock cube, then bring to a simmer, stirring to dissolve the stock cube and mix in the gochujang. Remove from the heat.

5 Spread the miso butter on the cut side of the cabbage. Place the cabbage in the middle of the beans, cut-side up, and cover the skillet with a lid or foil.

6 Roast in the oven for 20 minutes, then serve.

DIAL IT UP!

Sprinkle with Crispy Rosemary Pangrattato (page 240) before serving, for extra crunch.

Add a dollop of Tofu Crème Fraîche (page 241) before serving.

Serves 1

Prep time:
10 minutes

Cooking time:
12 minutes

Portobello Steak Sandwich with Chimichurri

For the sandwich
1 ciabatta
1 tsp Dijon mustard
1 tbsp vegan mayonnaise
Large handful of wild rocket or watercress
Handful of salted crinkle-cut crisps
1 tsp olive oil
3 portobello mushrooms
½ tsp fine sea salt
½ tsp ground black pepper

For the chimichurri
8g fresh coriander, finely chopped
8g fresh parsley, finely chopped
1 small shallot, finely diced
1 small garlic clove, minced
Pinch of chilli flakes
1 tbsp red wine vinegar
2 tbsp extra-virgin olive oil
2 tsp lemon juice
¼ tsp fine sea salt

This is what I like to call a 'self-care sandwich'. It's quick to make but takes just enough work to make you feel like you're really doing yourself a favour. Any extra chimichurri can be kept in a jar in the fridge for your next sandwich emergency.

1 Slice the ciabatta in half and toast the cut sides in a dry frying pan over medium heat until golden and crisp.

2 Spread the Dijon mustard and vegan mayonnaise on the toasted ciabatta. Layer with wild rocket or watercress and a handful of crinkle-cut crisps.

3 In the same frying pan, heat the olive oil over high heat. Add the mushrooms, placing a heavy pan on top to press them down, which helps to release moisture and enhance browning.

4 Sear the mushrooms for a few minutes, season with salt and pepper, then flip and sear for another 3–5 minutes, or until nicely browned.

5 While the mushrooms cook, put the chimichurri ingredients in a small bowl. Stir to combine.

6 Slice the cooked mushrooms into chunks and layer them onto the sandwich. Drizzle generously with chimichurri, close the sandwich, and serve.

DIAL IT UP!

Season the mushrooms with a little Magic Roast Chicken Salt (page 244) while they sear for an intensely meaty flavour.

Serves 1

Prep time: 10 minutes

Cooking time: 20 minutes

Cauliflower Schnitzel with Caper Butter Green Beans

For the cauliflower schnitzel
1cm thick wedge of cauliflower
2 tbsp plain flour
100ml unflavoured, unsweetened plant milk
1 tsp fine sea salt
½ tsp smoked paprika
1 tsp lemon juice
50g golden breadcrumbs
Cooking oil spray or vegetable oil

For the beans
100g fine green beans
40g vegan butter
1 shallot, finely chopped
2 tsp capers, drained
1 tsp Dijon mustard
Juice of ½ lemon
Pinch of flaky sea salt

People are apparently still really mad about vegans making 'cauliflower steaks' a thing, so in the hope of burying the hatchet, I promise to never use cauliflower in that way again... Instead I'll just use it for schnitzel! The cauliflower steak is dead; long live the cauliflower schnitzel!

1 Wash the cauliflower wedge and shake off any excess water. Dust it evenly with flour, ensuring all sides are lightly coated.

2 In a wide shallow bowl, mix the plant milk, fine sea salt, smoked paprika and lemon juice until well combined.

3 Dunk the cauliflower wedge into the plant milk mixture, coating it completely. Then press it into the breadcrumbs, ensuring an even layer covers all sides. Sprinkle breadcrumbs into any cracks or crevices that are uncoated.

4 Spray the breaded cauliflower lightly with spray oil or drizzle it with vegetable oil. Place in an air fryer and cook at 200°C for 20 minutes.

5 Meanwhile, heat a dry frying pan over medium heat until hot. Add the green beans and 3 tablespoons water, then cover with a lid.

6 Steam the beans for about 3 minutes, or until tender and the water has evaporated. Remove the beans from the pan and set aside.

7 Add the vegan butter to the same pan. Once melted, add the chopped shallot and capers. Fry for 3-4 minutes, stirring frequently, until the shallot softens and the capers start crackling and popping.

8 Remove the pan from the heat and whisk in the mustard, lemon juice and salt until the mixture is smooth and creamy. Return the beans to the pan and toss to coat.

9 Serve the crispy cauliflower schnitzel alongside the green beans. Drizzle any extra caper butter over the schnitzel before serving.

Serves 1

Prep time:
5 minutes

Cooking time:
15 minutes

Bombay Butter Beans

1 tbsp olive oil
2 green bird's eye chillies, left whole
½ tsp black mustard seeds
1 shallot, diced
1 tbsp ginger paste (or peeled and grated fresh ginger)
1 garlic clove, crushed
2 tsp garam masala
½ tsp ground turmeric
1 tbsp tomato purée
2 tsp mango chutney
150g cherry tomatoes
1 x 400g can butter beans, drained
½ tsp fine sea salt

For serving
Paratha (or roti or vegan naan)
3 tbsp vegan crème fraîche or unsweetened vegan yoghurt
Fresh coriander, roughly chopped
Squeeze of lemon juice

I'm a *big* fan of canned beans. You know how some people get anxious when their phone battery drops below 50 per cent? Well, I feel the same way when my canned bean shelf starts to look empty. They're such an easy win when it comes to quick dinners, and this recipe is one of my MVPs. It's based loosely on Bombay potatoes, but with big, creamy butterbeans instead of spuds.

1 In a frying pan, heat the olive oil over medium heat. Add the green chillies and mustard seeds, allowing them to temper until the mustard seeds begin to pop.

2 Add the shallot, ginger paste and garlic. Fry until the onion is softened and fragrant, about 5 minutes.

3 Stir in the spices, tomato purée, mango chutney and cherry tomatoes, followed by 200ml water.

4 Simmer, uncovered, for 8 minutes, or until the sauce has reduced and the cherry tomatoes have burst. Add the drained beans and fine sea salt and cook for a further 2 minutes until the beans are coated in a thick, rich tomato sauce.

5 While the beans cook, warm the roti or naan by heating in the microwave for 30 seconds or by toasting in a separate dry frying pan.

6 Transfer the beans to a serving bowl and gently stir in the vegan crème fraîche (or vegan yoghurt, if using). Top with fresh coriander and a squeeze of lemon and serve with a paratha.

Serves 1

Prep time:
5 minutes

Cooking time:
20 minutes

Definitely Not a Lasagne

- 1 tbsp olive oil
- 75g tempeh, broken into small chunks
- 1 tsp dark soy sauce
- ½ tsp smoked paprika
- 1 shallot, diced
- 1 garlic clove, minced
- 1 tbsp tomato purée
- 1 tsp miso paste
- 100ml passata
- 450ml boiling water
- 1 tsp vegan bouillon powder
- 1 tsp dried Italian herbs
- ¼ tsp chilli flakes
- ¼ tsp ground black pepper
- Pinch of flaky sea salt
- 4 lasagne sheets, broken into pieces (or 75g any broken pasta)
- 3 tbsp vegan crème fraîche (store-bought or see page 243)
- 1 tsp fresh parsley, basil or chives, for serving

This recipe is definitely *not* a lasagne. The flavours are bang on, but it's missing the layers, you know? But it's also not a lasagne soup, right? It's much more substantial than that. It's essentially a very saucy bowl of pasta that's based on and inspired by the true story of lasagne, but some characters have been renamed for legal reasons.

1. In a medium saucepan, heat ½ tablespoon of the olive oil over medium heat. Add the tempeh and fry for 3 minutes, stirring often, until lightly browned.
2. Transfer the tempeh to a small bowl, stir in the soy sauce and smoked paprika and set aside.
3. Add the remaining olive oil to the saucepan and fry the shallot and garlic for 2 minutes.
4. Add the tomato purée, miso paste, passata, boiling water, bouillon powder, Italian herbs, chilli flakes, black pepper and a pinch of flaky sea salt. Bring to the boil, then simmer for 5 minutes.
5. Add the broken lasagne sheets (or pasta pieces) and tempeh and cook for a further 10 minutes, stirring often, or until the pasta is al dente and the sauce has thickened nicely.
6. Transfer to a serving bowl and top with the vegan crème fraîche and fresh herbs. Serve hot.

Serves 1

Prep time:
5 minutes

Cooking time:
8 minutes

Courgette and Green Bean Stir Fry

Courgettes and green beans are probably the most chronically overcooked vegetable in British cuisine (and that's saying something). Courgettes, sliced into thick batons, need no more than three minutes in a hot wok, while green beans just need a bit of steam to get them bright green and tender. This makes them perfect for a light veggie stir fry that takes less than 15 minutes to make.

For the sauce
½ tsp toasted sesame oil
2 tbsp light soy sauce
1 tbsp rice vinegar (or white wine vinegar)
1 tbsp maple syrup
1 tsp cornflour
1 garlic clove, minced
¼ tsp chilli flakes (optional)

For the stir fry
½ tbsp vegetable oil
1 shallot, finely sliced
1 garlic clove, finely sliced
80g fine green beans, trimmed and halved
1 courgette (about 150g), chopped into 5mm thick batons

For serving
Steamed rice or noodles
Sesame seeds

1 Whisk together the sesame oil, soy sauce, rice vinegar, maple syrup, cornflour, minced garlic and chilli flakes (if using) in a small bowl. Set aside.

2 Heat a wok over high heat, then add the vegetable oil. Add the shallot, sliced garlic and green beans, stirring constantly for 1 minute. Pour in 1 tablespoon water, cover with a lid and steam for another minute, or until the water has evaporated.

3 Add the courgette and stir fry for 3 minutes until lightly browned but still holding its shape. The green beans should be blistered in spots.

4 Remove from the heat, pour in the sauce and stir to coat.

5 Serve immediately over steamed rice or noodles, sprinkled with sesame seeds.

DIAL IT UP!

Drizzle with some Crispy Garlic Chilli Oil (page 245) before serving.

Beef up the sauce with a teaspoon of Ultimate Umami Paste (page 243).

Serves 1

Prep time: 5 minutes

Cooking time: variable (see method)

Sticky Hoisin Tempeh Ribs

2 tbsp hoisin sauce
1 tbsp ginger paste
1 garlic clove, minced
1 tsp dark soy sauce
1 tsp rice vinegar
2 tsp brown sugar
½ tsp toasted sesame oil
150g tempeh, sliced into rib-like strips (If you can find smoked tempeh, use it! It's delicious)

For serving
150g cooked brown rice (use a microwave pouch if you're in a hurry)
¼ cucumber, finely sliced
1 spring onion, finely sliced
1 tbsp salted peanuts, crushed
½ red chilli, sliced
Small bunch of fresh coriander

You can make these tempeh ribs in a frying pan, an oven or an air fryer. I've not listed it here, but you can also cook them on the barbecue. Keep them in the marinade while you fire up the grill and cook until browned all over. If you're serving with rice, you'll find cooking times and methods in the cheat sheet on page 18.

1 In a medium bowl, whisk together the hoisin sauce, ginger paste, garlic, soy sauce, rice vinegar, brown sugar, sesame oil and 2 tablespoons water. Add the tempeh strips and toss them in the marinade.

2 **Frying option:** Place a small, dry frying pan over medium heat. Transfer the tempeh to the hot pan, shaking off any excess marinade back into the bowl as you go. Cook until browned on all sides, around 10 minutes, flipping occasionally to ensure it cooks evenly. Once the tempeh is browned, remove the pan from the heat and immediately stir in the remainder of the marinade from the bowl. It will bubble and thicken to a sticky glaze.

Oven option: Preheat the oven to 240°C/Fan 220°C/Gas Mark 9. Bake the tempeh on a lined tray for 15-18 minutes, flipping halfway through cooking. While the ribs bake, pour the marinade into a saucepan and bring to a simmer. Cook until thickened to a sticky glaze.

Air fryer option: Air fry the tempeh at 200°C for 15 minutes, shaking halfway through cooking. While the ribs cook, add the marinade to a saucepan and bring to a simmer. Cook until thickened to a sticky glaze.

3 Serve the tempeh ribs and their glaze with cooked brown rice and cucumber slices. Top with the spring onions, crushed peanuts, sliced chilli and coriander.

Serves 1

Prep time:
10 minutes

Cooking time:
15 minutes

Air-Fryer Tofu Po'boy

For the tofu
150g extra-firm tofu, drained
2 tbsp soy milk
1 tsp hot sauce, plus optional extra to serve
1 tsp soy sauce
1 tsp lemon juice
50g golden breadcrumbs

For the remoulade
2 tbsp vegan mayonnaise
1 tsp Dijon mustard
Dash of hot sauce
⅛ tsp garlic powder or granules
⅛ tsp onion powder
1 small shallot, finely chopped
1 tsp lemon juice
⅛ tsp fine sea salt
¼ tsp Cajun seasoning
Grind of black pepper

For the sandwich
1 vegan sub sandwich roll or ½ French baguette
A handful of shredded iceberg lettuce
1 tomato, sliced
¼ red onion, finely sliced

I first had a po'boy in New Orleans a few years ago and was immediately on board. It was packed with breaded tofu (in place of the traditional shrimp) and the most deliciously tangy, sweet remoulade. I've done my best to replicate that sandwich here for you, to help you jazz up your week. Get it? Jazz?

1 Set the air fryer to 200°C.

2 Break the tofu into bite-sized chunks and place them in a medium bowl. Add the soy milk, hot sauce, soy sauce, and lemon juice, and toss to coat.

3 Put the breadcrumbs in a separate shallow bowl.

4 Transfer the tofu to the breadcrumbs and toss again to coat. Place in the air fryer and cook until golden brown and crispy, about 15 minutes.

5 Meanwhile, make the remoulade by mixing together all the ingredients in a bowl - you can reuse the soy milk bowl to save on washing up.

6 Slice the sub roll in half and spread both cut sides with the remoulade. Top with shredded lettuce, tomato and sliced red onion, followed by the air-fried tofu. Serve with optional hot sauce on the side.

DIAL IT UP!

Swap the red onion for Pickled Pink Onions (page 246).

Swap the golden breadcrumbs for Crispy Rosemary Pangrattato (page 240) for a Mediterranean twist.

NUTRITION INFORMATION

Serves 1

Prep time:
5 minutes

Cooking time:
9 minutes

Quick Curry Udon for One

2 tsp vegetable oil
1 shallot, roughly chopped
80g tempeh, crumbled into small pieces
1 small carrot, peeled and sliced into 5mm dice
400ml vegetable stock
200g vacuum-packed udon noodles
1 Japanese curry block (about 18g)

For serving
1 spring onion, chopped
Pickled sushi ginger
1 sheet sushi nori, finely sliced

Big slurpy noodles in a rich Japanese curry sauce, spiked with pickled sushi ginger. To get curly spring onions like the ones in the picture, slice them into 2.5cm lengths, then slice again into long thin strips. Place in a bowl of very cold water for a few minutes while you prepare the noodles and they'll curl up before your eyes.

1 Heat the vegetable oil in a small saucepan over medium heat. Fry the shallot, tempeh and carrot for 2 minutes.

2 Add the vegetable stock to the saucepan, cover and simmer for 5 minutes, or until the carrot is tender.

3 Add the udon noodles and cook for 2 minutes until heated through, then remove from the heat. Stir in the curry block until the sauce is creamy and thick.

4 Pour into a bowl and serve topped with spring onion, pickled sushi ginger and sliced sushi nori.

DIAL IT UP!

For some heat, drizzle with Crispy Garlic Chilli Oil (page 245).

Serves 1

Prep time:
5 minutes

Cooking time:
10 minutes

Stout and Mustard Rarebit with Apple Slaw

For the rarebit
2 thick slices of sourdough bread
15g vegan butter
1½ tbsp plain flour
40ml stout (make sure it's a vegan variety)
80ml unflavoured, unsweetened plant milk
2 tbsp nutritional yeast
1½ tsp miso paste
1 tsp English mustard
1 tsp apple cider vinegar
1 tsp vegan Worcestershire sauce

For the apple slaw
1 small apple, cored and finely julienned
20g sweetheart cabbage, finely shredded
1 tsp finely chopped fresh chives, plus extra to sprinkle
1 tsp finely chopped fresh parsley
1 tbsp natural and unsweetened vegan yoghurt
1 tbsp vegan mayonnaise
1 tsp apple cider vinegar
1 tsp wholegrain mustard
Pinch of fine sea salt

If you were looking for an excuse to eat toast for dinner, then this is it. I grew up on Welsh rarebit, so this is a super nostalgic one for me. The apple slaw is sweet and crunchy to balance out the savoury, cheesy sauce. The recipe makes plenty, because I know you'll want another slice.

1 Preheat the grill to high. Place the bread on a baking sheet and toast both sides lightly.

2 Meanwhile, place the vegan butter in a small saucepan and melt over medium heat. Whisk in the flour and cook for a minute to remove the raw flour taste.

3 Add the stout, little by little, whisking as you go. Follow with the remaining rarebit ingredients, whisking vigorously until smooth. Bring to a simmer and cook for 2-3 minutes, or until thickened, then remove from the heat.

4 Spread the mixture over the slices of toast, then return to the grill until browned and bubbling, around 5-7 minutes.

5 To make the slaw, mix together all the slaw ingredients in a medium bowl.

6 Serve the grilled rarebit with the slaw on the side and few more chives sprinkled over the top.

Serves 1

Prep time:
5 minutes

Cooking time:
15 minutes

Spicy Corn and Tomato Soup

For the soup
1 tsp olive oil
½ onion, finely chopped
1 garlic clove, minced
2 tsp miso paste (red is ideal but white or brown are great too)
1 tbsp tomato purée
½ tbsp chipotle paste
80g cherry tomatoes
100g sun-dried tomatoes, from a jar, drained and roughly chopped
½ tsp chilli flakes (I use ancho or chipotle)
½ tsp dried oregano
400ml vegetable stock
60g corn kernels (frozen, canned or fresh)

For serving
Ground black pepper
¼ hass avocado, peeled and diced
1 radish, finely sliced

Corn is incredibly easy and quick to cook, but it's not always so easy to make it feel like the star of the show. For this recipe, the sweetness of corn is balanced by smoky, spicy chipotle and mellow, umami tomatoes. It's ready in minutes but you'll be thinking about it for hours.

1 Place a small saucepan over medium heat and add the olive oil. When hot, add the onion and garlic and fry until starting to brown, about 3 minutes.

2 Add the miso, tomato purée, chipotle paste, cherry tomatoes and a splash of water to prevent the mixture burning, and simmer for a further minute.

3 Add all the remaining soup ingredients except the corn. Bring to a simmer and cook, uncovered, for 8 minutes.

4 Add the corn kernels and simmer for a further 2 minutes.

5 Top with black pepper, avocado and sliced radish.

DIAL IT UP!

For some smoky heat, add a spoonful of Cheat's Salsa Macha (page 247).

Serves 1

Prep time: 5 minutes

Cooking time: 10 minutes

Sick Day Soba Ramen

1 tsp vegetable oil
3 spring onions, chopped, green and white parts separated
1 garlic clove, minced
1½ tbsp ginger paste
½ tsp ground turmeric
450ml vegetable stock
60g dried soba noodles
3 frozen vegetable gyozas
½ tbsp light soy sauce
1 tsp white miso paste
Juice of ½ lime
30g fresh spinach, roughly chopped
3 tbsp drained canned sweetcorn
Fresh coriander or chives, to serve
Pickled sushi ginger, to serve

Bright with turmeric and packed with ginger, not to mention quick and easy to make - if anything's going to get you back on your feet, it's this soup.

1. In a small saucepan, heat the vegetable oil over medium heat and fry the white parts of the spring onions, the garlic and the ginger paste until fragrant, around 2 minutes. Stir in the turmeric.
2. Gradually pour in the vegetable stock, stirring as you go, and bring to a boil.
3. Add the dried soba noodles to the broth and cook until tender, around 5 minutes. For the last 3 minutes of cooking, add the frozen gyozas.
4. Stir in the soy sauce, miso paste and lime juice. Add the fresh spinach to the hot broth and let it wilt slightly.
5. Transfer the ramen to a deep bowl and top with the sweetcorn. Garnish with the green parts of the spring onions and fresh coriander or chives, and some pickled ginger. Serve hot.

DIAL IT UP!

If you can handle the heat, add a splash of Crispy Garlic Chilli Oil (page 245)!

Serves 1

Prep time:
5 minutes

Cooking time:
10 minutes

Buffalo Tofu Flatbread Pizza

2 tbsp mild hot sauce (Frank's Red Hot works best)
1 garlic clove, minced
1 tbsp olive oil
½ tsp English mustard
125g extra-firm tofu, drained and crumbled
1 store-bought flatbread or Greek-style pitta
50ml passata
1 tbsp roughly chopped pickled jalapeños
Pinch of flaky sea salt
High-Protein Ranch Dressing (page 241, or substitute with vegan crème fraîche - see page 241 or shop-bought), for drizzling
1 tbsp crispy onions
Small bunch of fresh chives, finely chopped

I made this pizza for my friend Kelly once and honestly, she *will not* shut up about it. I mean it, she brings it up every time I see her. Yes, it's amazing. Yes, the spicy tofu is perfectly balanced by the creamy ranch. No, I can't think of a better way to use a store-bought flatbread. *Alright?* Anyway, Kelly, here's the recipe so you can finally make it for yourself and we can *finally* talk about something else. Like those coconut noodles you made me once - OMG.

1 In a medium bowl, whisk together the hot sauce, garlic, olive oil and English mustard until smooth. Add the crumbled tofu and stir until evenly coated.

2 Preheat the grill to high. Spread the coated tofu on a baking sheet and grill for 5 minutes, or until lightly coloured.

3 Meanwhile, place the flatbread on a baking sheet and spread the passata evenly over the surface. Top with the grilled tofu and drizzle over any remaining buffalo sauce from the tofu bowl.

4 Sprinkle the chopped jalapeños over the pizza and season with a pinch of flaky sea salt. Grill for 5-10 minutes, or until the toppings are bubbling and the edges of the flatbread are golden.

5 Remove from the grill and drizzle with ranch dressing or vegan crème fraîche. Garnish with the crispy onions and chopped chives. Slice and serve immediately

(image on previous spread)

Serves 1

Prep time:
5 minutes

Cooking time:
10 minutes

Smoky Sobrasada Gnocchi

4 sun-dried tomatoes, finely chopped, plus a drizzle of oil from the jar
250g store-bought vegan gnocchi (I use De Cecco)
1 small garlic clove, minced
1 tbsp tomato purée
1 tsp red miso paste
½ tsp smoked paprika
200ml boiling water
2 tbsp nutritional yeast
Sea salt and ground black pepper
Fresh basil leaves, to serve

Sobrasada is a kind of spicy sausage, popular on the Balearic Islands in Spain. It's obviously not vegan, but the flavour can be mimicked pretty closely with sun-dried tomatoes and spices. Since the sausages are cured, I also use red miso to give that funky fermented umami flavour.

1 Heat a non-stick frying pan over medium heat and add a drizzle of olive oil from the sun-dried tomato jar. Add the gnocchi in a single layer and pan-fry for 5 minutes, shaking the pan occasionally, until golden and crispy on all sides.

2 Push the gnocchi to one side of the pan. Add the garlic, sun-dried tomatoes, tomato purée, red miso paste, smoked paprika, a small pinch of salt and black pepper and 200ml boiling water to the empty space. Cook for 2 minutes until fragrant.

3 Stir together the contents of the pan, then sprinkle the nutritional yeast over the mixture and stir again to create a smooth sauce that coats the gnocchi.

4 Taste and adjust seasoning if needed. Transfer to a bowl, garnish with torn fresh basil leaves and serve immediately.

(image overleaf)

DIAL IT UP!

Sprinkle with Crispy Rosemary Pangrattato (page 240) before serving for extra crunch.

Make-Ahead Meals

It's a Wednesday night, you've had a day so long it deserves its own Peter Jackson trilogy, and the last thing you want to do is wrestle with a chopping board while your stomach growls at you. This is precisely the moment when Past You - organised, forward-thinking, borderline-saintly Past You - can step in and save the day. This chapter is a love letter to your future self, packed with game-changing vegan recipes that can be made in advance, stashed in the fridge or freezer, and resurrected just when you need them most. Think of it as meal prep, but for people who can't stand the idea of eating the same sad Tupperware dinner three days in a row.

I won't pretend that I always have my life together enough to be that forward-thinking - you and I have a rapport based on honesty and vulnerability and I don't want to jeopardise that. But when I do manage to get ahead of the chaos - when I open my fridge and find an actually edible, genuinely exciting vegan dinner waiting for me - I feel like I've hacked the system. It's like discovering that *not only* is there one last biscuit in the tin, but that it's a bloomin' dark chocolate Hobnob! Small victories! We deserve more of them.

So, whether you're stockpiling meals for a busy week or simply trying to avoid the dreaded 'What's for dinner?' meltdown, this chapter has got you covered. From Kale, Pistachio and Preserved Lemon Pesto (page 93) that you can jar up and store for your next bowl of panic pasta, to a dish of Shredded Tofu Enchiladas (page 92) straight from the freezer and tastier than ever, these recipes will make Future You look like an absolute genius.

Makes
4 flatbreads

Prep time:
20 minutes

Cooking time:
15 minutes

Mushroom Tikka Kebabs with Lime Pickle Yoghurt

For the mushrooms
2 garlic cloves, minced
1 tbsp ginger paste
1 tbsp garam masala
½ tsp mild chilli powder
½ tsp ground turmeric
100g vegan yoghurt
1 tbsp olive oil
1 tbsp mango chutney
1 tbsp lemon juice
2 tbsp gram flour (aka chickpea flour)
1 tsp fine sea salt
500g mushrooms (I use a mixture of chestnut and oyster mushrooms), roughly sliced

For the lime pickle yoghurt
150g vegan coconut yoghurt
1 tbsp lime pickle
1 tbsp lime juice
1 tsp maple syrup
1 tbsp finely chopped fresh coriander

For serving
4 flatbreads
200g red cabbage, shredded
Small bunch of fresh coriander, roughly chopped

The mushrooms in this recipe benefit greatly from a good, long marinade to really let the flavours develop. So, prepare these first, and if you're making this recipe in advance, pop them in the fridge before you go to work. They just need a quick bake until lightly crispy before serving, and you're ready to roll.

1 In a medium bowl, mix together the garlic, ginger paste, garam masala, chilli powder, turmeric, yoghurt, olive oil, mango chutney, lemon juice, gram flour and sea salt until smooth.

2 Add the sliced mushrooms to the bowl with the marinade. Stir gently to coat the mushrooms evenly.

3 In a separate bowl, combine the coconut yoghurt, lime pickle, lime juice, maple syrup and chopped coriander. If the lime pickle is very chunky, chop it finely before adding.

4 **If making ahead,** place the marinated mushrooms and lime pickle yoghurt in airtight containers and place in the fridge for up to 24 hours.

5 **To cook,** preheat the oven to 220°C/Fan 200°C/Gas Mark 7. Spread out the marinated mushrooms in an even layer on a baking tray. Bake for 20 minutes, turning over halfway through cooking. The mushrooms should be browned and slightly charred in places.

6 Warm the flatbreads in the microwave for 30 seconds, or as per the package instructions.

7 Spread some lime pickle yoghurt on each flatbread. Top with baked mushrooms, shredded red cabbage and a sprinkling of fresh coriander. Serve immediately.

Serves 4 | Prep time: 10 minutes | Cooking time: 35 minutes

Bourguignon Pot Pie

35g vegan butter
200g pearl shallots
800g mixed mushrooms, small ones left whole and large ones chopped into large chunks
2 tbsp olive oil
2 celery sticks, sliced into 5mm pieces
150g carrots, peeled and chopped into chunks
3 garlic cloves, minced
6 sprigs of fresh thyme, stems removed
2 tbsp tomato purée
2½ tbsp plain flour
160ml vegan red wine
300ml boiling vegetable stock
1 bay leaf
1 tbsp dark soy sauce
320g ready-rolled vegan puff pastry
Unflavoured, unsweetened plant milk, for brushing
Flaky sea salt and ground black pepper
Steamed vegetables, to serve

Mushrooms are the star of this insanely meaty pot pie, and I urge you strongly to use a varied selection such as some fresh shiitake, oyster or shimeji to keep the texture and flavour diverse!

1 Melt half of the butter in a large pot over medium heat. Sauté the shallots and half of the mushrooms until browned, around 5-7 minutes. Remove and set aside, then repeat with the remaining butter and mushrooms. Remove from the pot and set aside.

2 Add the olive oil, celery, carrots, garlic and thyme to the pot. Fry for a minute, then stir in the tomato purée and flour. Add the red wine and stir to deglaze the pot.

3 Bring to a simmer, then add the vegetable stock, bay leaf, dark soy sauce, the mushrooms and shallots, and season with salt and black pepper. Cover and allow to simmer for 10 minutes, stirring occasionally, until glossy and thickened.

4 Transfer the mixture to an oven-safe dish and allow to cool to room temperature.

5 Cut a circle of the rolled-out puff pastry slightly bigger than the top of the dish. Lay it over the dish and crimp the edges. Cut a steam hole in the centre.

6 **If making in advance,** wrap the dish with foil and place it in the freezer. Keep frozen for up to 3 months and defrost in the fridge overnight before baking.

7 **To bake,** preheat the oven to 220°C/Fan 200°C/Gas Mark 7. Brush the top of the pie with plant milk and place in the oven to bake for 25 minutes, or until the pastry is puffed and golden and the filling is piping hot.

8 Serve hot with fresh steamed vegetables.

DIAL IT UP!

Swap out the tomato purée for the same amount of Ultimate Umami Paste (page 243) for an even more intense mushroom flavour.

ALUMINIU

Makes
12 slices

Prep time:
10 minutes

Cooking time:
40 minutes

Roasting Tin Spanish Omelette with Mojo Verde

2 tbsp olive oil, plus extra for greasing
2 onions, peeled and cubed
750g new potatoes, cubed
450g extra-firm tofu
500ml unsweetened plant milk
1 tbsp white miso paste
½ tsp sea salt
¼ tsp ground black pepper
300g gram flour (aka chickpea flour)
1 red pepper, deseeded and diced
Small bunch of fresh parsley, roughly chopped
60g vegan feta, crumbled
Dried chilli flakes, to sprinkle
Leafy salad, to serve

For the mojo verde sauce
50g fresh coriander (leaves and stems)
1 garlic clove
1 tsp ground cumin
1 tbsp red wine vinegar
100ml olive oil
Juice of 1 lime
½ tsp sea salt
¼ tsp ground black pepper

My mum and dad spend a few months every year in the Canary Islands and over many visits, I've grown rather obsessed with Canarian *mojo verde*. It's a bright green sauce that's kind of halfway between a salsa verde and a delicious herb oil and is traditionally served with boiled potatoes, but I've paired it with a super simple baked tortilla that's great for weekly meal prep. Just bake, slice and reheat any time you need a quick, filling, high-protein dinner.

1 Preheat the oven to 220°C/Fan 200°C/Gas Mark 7. Lightly grease a large roasting tin (about 23 x 33cm) with olive oil.

2 Scatter the onions and new potatoes into the tin and drizzle with the olive oil, stirring to coat. Roast in the preheated oven for 20 minutes.

3 Meanwhile, in a high-speed blender, combine 250ml water with the tofu, plant milk, miso paste, sea salt and black pepper. Blend until smooth, then transfer to a large bowl. Add the gram flour and whisk until smooth.

4 Remove the roasted potatoes and onions from the oven and reduce the heat to 180°C/Fan 160°C/Gas Mark 4. Add the diced red pepper to the tin. Pour over the blended mixture and stir to combine, ensuring the veggies are evenly coated with the batter.

5 Top with the parsley, crumbled vegan feta and chilli flakes. Bake for 20 minutes, or until set and golden in places.

6 Meanwhile, make the mojo verde by blending all the ingredients in a blender or food processor until smooth.

7 **If serving now,** allow the omelette to cool slightly, then slice into 12 squares. Serve drizzled with the mojo verde sauce with a simple leafy salad on the side.

8 **If making ahead,** allow the omelette to cool to room temperature before transferring it to an airtight container. Store in the fridge for up to 3 days. The omelette can be served chilled or reheated in the microwave for 2 minutes before serving. *(image on previous spread)*

Makes
10 pasties

Prep time:
20 minutes

Cooking time:
40 minutes

Bonfire Pasties

½ swede (around 600g), peeled and sliced into 5mm cubes
2 carrots (around 150g), peeled and sliced into 5mm cubes
1 large potato (around 250g), peeled and sliced into 5mm cubes
Leaves from 6 sprigs of fresh thyme
1 tbsp finely chopped fresh parsley
1 vegan stock cube, crumbled
1 tsp dried sage
½ tsp ground black pepper
2 tbsp olive oil
100g frozen garden peas
3 tbsp caramelised red onion chutney
1 tsp Marmite, or Ultimate Umami Paste (page 243)
2 x 475g packs of pre-rolled shortcrust pastry
2 tbsp plant milk
1 tbsp maple syrup
1 tsp vegetable oil

In my house, it's mince pies for Christmas, Spanakopita for Easter and these Bonfire Pasties for Bonfire Night. Herby and warming, they can be made and frozen months ahead and baked up fresh, in time for huddling around a bonfire.

1 Preheat the oven to 220°C/Fan 200°C/Gas Mark 7. In a large bowl, toss the swede, carrots, potato, thyme, parsley, stock cube, sage and black pepper with the olive oil. Spread over a baking sheet and roast for 25 minutes, or until the vegetables are tender and slightly browned. Remove from the oven and reduce the temperature to 200°C/Fan 180°C/Gas Mark 6.

2 Stir the garden peas, red onion chutney and Marmite through the roasted vegetables, then set aside to cool.

3 Unroll the pastry and cut out 10 equal circles, roughly 12cm in diameter, using a cookie cutter or small plate as a guide.

4 Place 2 dessertspoons of the mixture in the centre of a circle of pastry. Wet the edge slightly with water, then fold over into a semi-circle, pinch the edges closed and crimp to seal. Repeat to fill the remaining pasties.

5 Place the pasties on lined baking sheets and make a steam hole in the centre of each with the tip of a sharp knife.

6 **If making in advance,** transfer the baking sheets to the freezer until the pasties are frozen solid, then transfer to an airtight container or freezer bag and keep frozen for up to 3 months. Allow to defrost fully before baking.

7 **To bake,** arrange the pasties on baking sheets lined with baking paper. (You'll need to preheat the oven to 200°C/ Fan 180°C/Gas Mark 6 again if you have made these ahead and frozen them.) Make the pastry wash by whisking together the plant milk, maple syrup and vegetable oil, then brush onto the pasties. Bake for 30 minutes, brushing again with the wash halfway through baking and immediately after baking.

8 Allow to cool slightly before serving. *(image overleaf)*

Serves 2

Prep time:
15 minutes

Cooking time:
25 minutes

Crispy Rice Paper Dumplings in Chilli Vinegar

For the dumplings
2 tbsp vegetable oil
2 garlic cloves, crushed
4 spring onions, finely chopped
250g fresh shiitake mushrooms, finely chopped
160g medium-firm tofu, drained and crumbled
½ tsp ground black pepper
2 tbsp soy sauce
10 rice paper sheets (the kind used for summer rolls)

For the chilli vinegar
2 tbsp soy sauce
2 tbsp Chinese black vinegar or balsamic vinegar
2 tsp sesame oil
1 tsp sugar
2 tsp Crispy Garlic Chilli Oil (page 245), or store-bought crispy chilli oil

For serving
½ cucumber, finely sliced
1 spring onion, finely chopped
White sesame seeds

My local international supermarket used to sell a particular brand of frozen vegan dumplings that I was totally obsessed with. Then, one day, *poof!* They disappeared. None of the staff knew what I was talking about - one guy even tried to gaslight me into thinking I'd dreamt them up. So, in desperation, I decided to make them myself. Just like the 'made-up' ones, mine are packed with meaty, minced shiitakes and aromatic spring onions. These ones freeze perfectly too, and when fried, they're crispy outside and super juicy inside. Drizzle with homemade chilli vinegar and you've got a delicious dinner based on a product I may or may not have imagined entirely.

1 Heat 1 tablespoon of the vegetable oil in a large frying pan. Add the garlic, spring onions and shiitake mushrooms. Fry until the mushrooms have released all their moisture and are starting to brown, around 3 minutes. Add the tofu and black pepper and mix well, breaking up any large crumbles with the spatula. Cook for a further 2 minutes, then remove from the heat and stir the soy sauce through. Set aside and allow to cool.

2 Dunk a rice paper sheet in a bowl of water a few times, then lay it flat on a clean work surface. Spoon around 1 dessertspoon of the mixture into the centre of the rice paper. Fold the left side over the filling, followed by the right side. Finally, fold up the bottom and roll up to completely wrap the filling. Transfer to a plate and repeat with the remaining filling and rice paper sheets.

3 **If making in advance,** place the plate of dumplings in the freezer until solid, then transfer to a freezer-proof container and keep frozen for up to 3 months. Allow to defrost fully before cooking.

(recipe continues overleaf)

4 **To cook,** heat a large frying pan over medium heat and add the remaining tablespoon of vegetable oil. Place the dumplings in the hot oil, making sure they're not touching (or they'll stick together), and fry until browned on all sides, around 10-12 minutes.

5 In a small bowl, whisk together the chilli vinegar ingredients.

6 Divide the crispy dumplings between two bowls and drizzle with the chilli vinegar. Serve with sliced cucumber, sprinkled with the sliced spring onions and sesame seeds.

Serves 6

Prep time:
20 minutes

Cooking time:
55 minutes

Cottage Pie Jacket Potatoes

6 large baking potatoes
40g vegan butter
6 tbsp plant milk
Sea salt and ground black pepper
Veggies or salad, to serve (optional)

For the filling
2 x 400g cans green lentils, drained and rinsed
1 tbsp olive oil, plus extra for drizzling
2 vegetable stock cubes, crumbled
2 tbsp tomato purée
2 tbsp ketchup
2 tsp maple syrup
2 tsp dark soy sauce
2 tsp Dijon mustard
2 tsp miso paste (ideally red)
2 tsp dried parsley
1 tsp dried thyme
½ tsp garlic powder
1 tsp vegan Worcestershire sauce
200g mixed frozen veg

When I bake jacket potatoes, I always bake too many. It's because they take so long to bake perfectly, I always feel like I should batch cook a whole bunch. But who wants to eat a whole batch of jacket potatoes (besides Brian Harvey, famously)? If you're like me, then this recipe is a great way to use up excess jackets by turning them into individual cottage pies. They freeze perfectly and can be baked from frozen, so if you ask me, they're the perfect recipe mash-up. I said *mash* up. Never mind.

1 Preheat the oven to 200°C/Fan 180°C/Gas Mark 6, if baking today.

2 Prick the potatoes with a fork and microwave on high for 25 minutes, turning halfway through, until soft and cooked through.

3 Meanwhile, in a medium bowl, mix together all the filling ingredients.

4 When the potatoes are cooked, allow to cool slightly, then slice off the tops and carefully scoop out the middles, leaving enough flesh on each to give six sturdy shells.

5 Peel the skin from the sliced-off potato tops and discard, and place the flesh in a medium bowl with the scooped-out potato middles. Add the vegan butter and soy milk and mash until smooth. Season with salt and pepper to taste.

6 Divide the filling evenly among the potato shells. Spoon the mashed potato topping over the filling and drizzle with a little extra olive oil.

7 **To bake,** place the filled potatoes on a baking tray and bake in the preheated oven for 30 minutes, or until the tops are golden and slightly crispy and the filling is bubbling hot.

(recipe continues overleaf)

8 **If making in advance,** place the filled potatoes on a baking tray and place in the freezer until frozen solid. Transfer to an airtight container and keep frozen for up to 3 months. To bake from frozen, preheat the oven to 200°C/Fan 180°C/ Gas Mark 6. Place the filled potatoes on a baking tray and bake in the preheated oven for 40 minutes, or until the tops are golden and slightly crispy and the filling is bubbling hot.

9 Serve hot on their own or with a side of your favourite veggies or mixed salad.

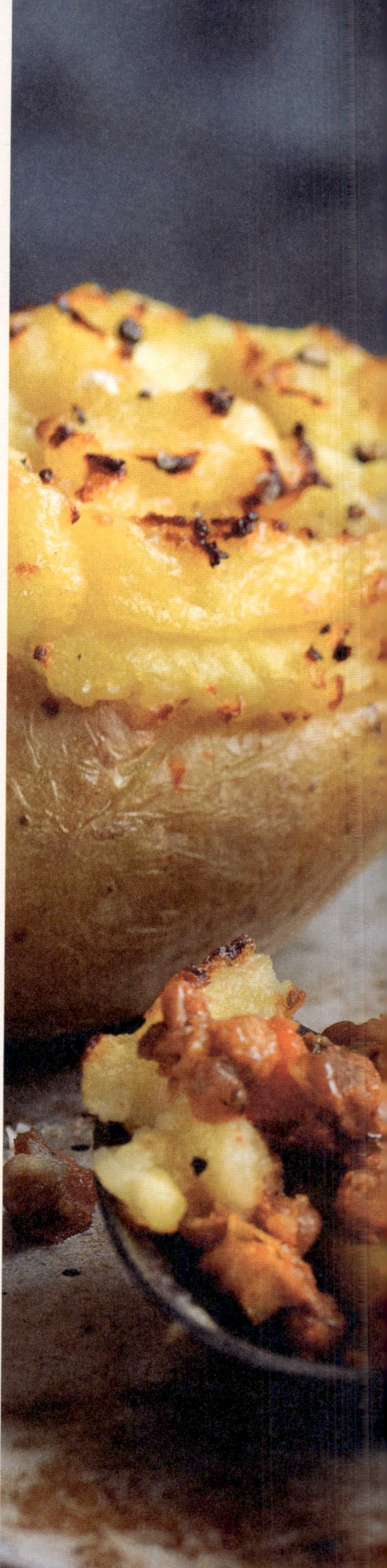

Serves 4

Prep time:
10 minutes

Cooking time:
30 minutes

Roasted Cauliflower Soup

For the roasted cauliflower
750g cauliflower (around 1 head), cut into florets
1 tbsp olive oil
3 garlic cloves, crushed
1 tsp dried thyme
Pinch of cayenne pepper
20g nutritional yeast
Pinch of flaky sea salt
½ tsp ground black pepper

For the soup
1 tbsp olive oil
1 large onion, roughly chopped
1 celery stalk, roughly chopped
1 litre boiling water
2 stock cubes
2 tbsp miso paste
1 tbsp Dijon mustard
150g silken tofu
2 tbsp lemon juice
Crispy Garlic Chilli Oil (page 245), to serve
Chopped fresh chives or thyme, to serve

Nutritional yeast is the magic ingredient in this super-cheesy cauliflower soup recipe. 'Nooch' is already a pretty cheesy-tasting ingredient, but I figured out that if you roast it, the flavour becomes so much more intense. Combine with umami-rich miso paste and tangy lemon juice and the cheesy vibes hit critical levels.

1 Preheat your oven to 220°C/Fan 200°C/Gas Mark 7.

2 Toss the cauliflower florets with the olive oil, garlic, dried thyme, cayenne pepper, nutritional yeast, flaky sea salt, and black pepper in a large bowl.

3 Spread the cauliflower evenly on a baking tray and roast for 25 minutes, flipping halfway through cooking, until golden and tender.

4 While the cauliflower roasts, heat the olive oil for the soup in a large pot over medium heat. Add the onion and celery, and sauté for 6–8 minutes until softened and translucent.

5 Add the roasted cauliflower (reserving a few florets for topping), along with the boiling water, stock cubes, miso paste and mustard. Stir to combine and bring to a simmer. Cover with a lid and allow to cook for 10 minutes.

6 Remove the pot from the heat and add the silken tofu and lemon juice.

7 Blend the soup using an immersion blender until smooth and creamy. If the soup is too thick, add a little more boiling water to reach your desired consistency. Taste and adjust the seasoning with additional salt, pepper, or lemon juice, if needed.

(recipe continues overleaf)

8 **If serving now,** ladle the soup into bowls, garnish with the reserved roasted cauliflower, a drizzle of chilli oil and fresh chives or thyme.

9 **If serving later,** allow the soup to cool to room temperature, then transfer to an airtight container and store in the fridge for up to 2 days. The miso paste in the recipe means the flavour will develop over time! Alternatively, transfer individual portions of soup to airtight freezer-safe containers and freeze for up to 3 months. Defrost before reheating in a saucepan over medium heat or in the microwave until piping hot.

Serves 2 | Prep time: 20 minutes | Cooking time: 16 minutes

Red Curry Fishless Cakes with Peanut Slaw

For the fishless cakes
1 x 400g can hearts of palm, drained and roughly chopped
150g medium-firm tofu, drained
2 spring onions, finely chopped
1 tbsp vegan red curry paste
1 tsp ginger paste, or freshly grated ginger
1 garlic clove, minced
1 tsp brown sugar
Zest of ½ lime, finely grated
Small bunch of fresh coriander, chopped
3 tbsp plain flour, plus extra for dusting
1 tbsp vegetable oil
Lime wedges, to serve

For the peanut slaw
50g shredded red cabbage
50g shredded white cabbage
1 small carrot, peeled and sliced into matchsticks
50g cooked edamame beans
1 spring onion, finely chopped
40g salted peanuts, roughly chopped
1 tbsp agave syrup
1 tbsp rice vinegar or lime juice
1 tbsp olive oil
1 tbsp soy sauce
1 tbsp peanut butter
2 tsp sriracha
1 tsp ginger paste

This recipe is for my mum. She went vegan not long after I did, back in 2017, and although she doesn't say it explicitly, I *know* that she misses seafood. She also loves Thai food, so it's a win-win! These fishless cakes are gently spiced and super fragrant, with a light, flaky texture. They're also freezable, and because they're dinky, they don't need to be defrosted before frying.

1 Place the chopped hearts of palm and the tofu on a clean kitchen towel (or in a nut milk bag) and wring out as much moisture as possible. The tofu will get mushed up - this is what you want.

2 Transfer the hearts of palm and tofu to a large bowl. Add the spring onions, red curry paste, ginger, garlic, brown sugar, lime zest, coriander and flour. Mix everything together thoroughly with your hands until well combined.

3 Form the mixture into six patties and carefully dust the outsides with the extra flour.

4 **If making in advance,** place the patties on a small baking sheet and freeze until solid. Transfer them to an airtight container or zip-lock bag and freeze for up to 2 months.

5 **To cook,** heat a large frying pan over medium heat and add the vegetable oil. Fry the patties for 5-8 minutes on each side, or until gently browned (you'll need to add a few minutes to this if cooking from frozen).

6 While the fishless cakes cook, combine the red cabbage, white cabbage, carrot matchsticks, edamame, spring onion and chopped peanuts in a large bowl.

7 In a separate small bowl, whisk together the agave syrup, rice vinegar (or lime juice), olive oil, soy sauce, peanut butter, sriracha and ginger paste to make the dressing.

8 Pour half of this dressing over the slaw and toss to coat.

9 Serve the fishless cakes with the peanut slaw on the side. Garnish with lime wedges and the remaining dressing for dipping

Serves 8

Prep time:
30 minutes

Cooking time:
30 minutes

Mushroom Quinoa Burgers

1 tbsp olive oil
150g chestnut mushrooms, finely chopped or shredded using a box grater
150g shiitake mushrooms, finely chopped or shredded using a box grater
1 x 250g pouch microwave quinoa
50ml dry white wine, or water
1 vegetable stock cube
350g firm tofu
3 tbsp plain white flour
1 tbsp dark soy sauce
1 tbsp tomato purée
2 tsp vegan Worcestershire sauce
¼ tsp fine sea salt
½ tsp ground black pepper

For serving
Quick Ketchup (page 242)
8 burger buns, halved
3 tomatoes, sliced
1 avocado, peeled, pitted and sliced
1 head lettuce
Sliced pickles (optional)

I know what you're thinking: 'Do we really need another vegan burger?' Well, this one is minimally processed and yet still packed with plant-based protein and loads of flavour. It's freezable for convenience *and* it's baked, not fried. So yes! I think the answer is yes: there is life *beyond* the Beyond burger!

1 Heat the olive oil in a large frying pan over medium heat. Once hot, add the chestnut and shiitake mushrooms. Cook, stirring frequently, for about 5–7 minutes, or until the mushrooms release their moisture and begin to brown slightly.

2 Add the quinoa directly to the pan, breaking it up with a spoon. Pour in the dry white wine (or water) and crumble in the vegetable stock cube. Stir everything together well to combine, then allow it to cook for another 5 minutes, stirring occasionally, until most of the liquid has been absorbed. Transfer this mixture to a plate or shallow dish and spread it out to cool completely.

3 While the mushroom and quinoa mixture cools, wrap the tofu in a nut milk bag, clean cloth or kitchen paper, and squeeze firmly to remove as much moisture as possible. Transfer to a large mixing bowl and mash thoroughly with a fork until the tofu resembles a chunky paste.

4 Once the mushroom and quinoa mixture has cooled, add it to the bowl with the mashed tofu. Add all the remaining burger ingredients. Mix together to form a chunky dough that holds together when pressed.

5 Divide the mixture into eight equal portions. Roll each portion into a ball, then gently flatten it into a burger patty about 1cm thick.

(recipe continues overleaf)

6 **To freeze for later,** Arrange the patties in a single layer on a baking sheet lined with baking paper and freeze until solid, about 30 minutes. Once frozen, transfer the patties to an airtight container or zip-lock bag and store in the freezer for up to 3 months. Defrost completely before cooking.

7 **To cook,** preheat the oven to 220°C/Fan 200°C/Gas Mark 7. Line a baking sheet with baking paper and place the burgers on the sheet, spacing them evenly. Bake the patties for 30 minutes, flipping them carefully halfway through cooking to ensure both sides are evenly browned.

8 Spread a generous layer of ketchup on the bottom half of each bun, place a cooked burger patty on top, followed by slices of tomato and avocado, lettuce leaves and pickles, if using. Finish with the top half of the bun and serve.

Serves 2

Prep time: 5 minutes

Cooking time: 25 minutes

Pho Now or Pho Later

1 tsp vegetable oil
200g extra-firm tofu, drained and cubed
2 shallots, roughly chopped
2 garlic cloves, peeled and roughly crushed with the side of a knife
2.5cm piece of ginger, roughly sliced
2 star anise
4 whole cloves
2 tsp coriander seeds
2 cardamom pods
1 cinnamon stick
½ tsp chilli flakes
½ tsp fennel seeds
1.5 litres vegetable stock
150g long-stem broccoli, ends trimmed
170g flat rice noodles
1 tbsp soy sauce
1 tbsp brown sugar
1 tsp fine sea salt
2 tbsp white rice vinegar

For serving
1 shallot, finely chopped
1 red chilli, deseeded and finely chopped
1 carrot, peeled and julienned or grated
Fresh coriander, mint and basil
2 wedges of lime

The best bit about Pho, IMO, is the broth. Unfortunately, it's also the most time-consuming part. But don't fret! I've streamlined the process for you *and* made sure that it's suitable for meal prep! The broth can sit in the fridge for up to a week, ready to be reheated and poured over noodles and veggies at a moment's notice. And because it's full of spices and aromatics, it'll even taste better with time!

1 Heat the vegetable oil in a large saucepan over medium heat. Fry the tofu for 5 minutes or until browned, then remove it from the pan and set aside.

2 Add the shallots, garlic, ginger and spices to the pan and cook for 2 minutes until fragrant. Slowly pour in the vegetable stock, taking care to avoid splashing, and bring it to the boil over medium heat. Let it boil for 10 minutes.

3 Place the broccoli in a sieve or steamer basket and position it over the simmering pot. Cover with a lid and steam for 5 minutes or until tender. Remove the broccoli and set aside.

4 Strain the broth to remove the spices and aromatics, then return the clear broth to the pan over medium heat. Add the flat rice noodles and cook in the broth for 5 minutes, or until tender.

5 Divide the noodles between two deep bowls, topping them with the steamed broccoli and fried tofu.

6 Stir the soy sauce, brown sugar and white rice vinegar into the hot broth, then remove it from the heat.

(recipe continues overleaf)

7 **If serving now,** pour the seasoned broth over the noodles, broccoli and tofu in each bowl.

8 **If serving later,** allow the broth to cool to room temperature before transferring to an airtight container. Cover the bowls of noodles, broccoli and tofu (or transfer them to a heat-proof jar) and store in the fridge for up to a week. When ready to serve, bring the broth to the boil again and pour over the noodles.

9 Garnish with the chopped shallot, red chilli, julienned carrot, fresh herbs and a lime wedge before serving.

DIAL IT UP!

Boost the spice levels with a drizzle of Crispy Garlic Chilli Oil (page 245).

Serves 4

Prep time: 10 minutes

Cooking time: 20 minutes

Tempeh Tikka Masala

- 2 tbsp olive oil
- 1 large onion, roughly chopped
- 3 garlic cloves, minced
- 2.5cm piece of ginger, peeled and grated
- 1 tbsp garam masala
- 1 tsp ground coriander
- 2 tsp ground cumin
- 1 tsp ground turmeric
- ¼ tsp chilli powder
- Small bunch of fresh coriander, plus extra to serve
- 1 tbsp mango chutney
- 400g tempeh (or substitute with extra-firm tofu, if preferred), cubed
- 2 tbsp tomato purée
- 1 x 400g can chopped tomatoes
- Juice of ½ lemon
- 200g vegan coconut yoghurt
- Sea salt
- Cooked rice or roti, for serving

This is my husband's second favourite dinner (second only to a roast dinner, which is saying something). It's also the recipe that took him from tempeh sceptic to tempeh yep-tic (OK, that one needs workshopping). I like to portion up a bunch of meals and freeze in airtight containers so they're ready to go at a moment's notice. He thinks I'm a supernaturally fast cook, but if you're reading this, Peter, I'm just a freezer hoarder.

1 Preheat the grill to high.

2 Blend 1 tablespoon of the olive oil, the onion, garlic, ginger, ground spices, fresh coriander, mango chutney, and 120ml of water into a paste. Set aside.

3 Toss the tempeh with half the paste, ensuring it is well coated but remains intact. Spread it on a baking sheet and grill on the top shelf of the oven for 20 minutes, flipping halfway through cooking, until browned on the edges.

4 Heat the remaining olive oil in a frying pan over medium heat. Cook the remaining paste with the tomato purée for 3-5 minutes until thick and deep red.

5 Add the chopped tomatoes and half a can of water. Bring to a simmer, cover and cook for 15 minutes, stirring occasionally, until the sauce thickens. Remove from the heat and stir in the lemon juice and vegan coconut yoghurt.

6 Add the grilled tempeh to the sauce. Season with salt to taste.

7 **If serving now,** top with fresh coriander and serve with rice or roti.

8 **If serving later,** allow the dish to cool completely, then freeze it in an airtight container for up to 3 months. Defrost overnight in the fridge. Reheat gently in a pan over medium heat, adding water if needed to adjust the consistency.

Serves 4

Prep time:
10 minutes

Cooking time:
45 minutes

Shredded Tofu Enchiladas

For the shredded tofu filling
450g extra-firm tofu, drained
1 red pepper, sliced
1 red onion, sliced
2 tbsp olive oil
2 tsp ground cumin
1 tsp ground coriander
2 tsp chipotle chilli paste
2 tsp smoked paprika
1 tsp garlic powder
½ tsp mild chilli powder
1 tsp dried oregano
150g passata
2 tbsp tomato purée
1 tbsp soy sauce
1 tbsp brown sugar

For the enchilada sauce
1 tbsp olive oil
2 tbsp plain flour
1 tbsp smoked paprika
½ tsp garlic powder
1 tsp ground cumin
1 tsp ground coriander
½ tsp dried oregano
400ml vegetable stock
1 tbsp tomato purée
200g passata
½ tsp fine sea salt
1 tsp white wine vinegar

To assemble and serve
8 small flour or corn tortillas
150g Tofu Crème Fraîche (page 241), or vegan yoghurt
Fresh coriander, chopped
Red onion, finely sliced
50g vegan feta, crumbled

This one's rather heavy on the number of ingredients, compared to the rest of the book, but I promise you it's worth it. It's truly up there with the most impressive freezer-friendly dinners.

1 Preheat your oven to 220°C/Fan 200°C/Gas Mark 7.

2 Drain the tofu and shred it into a large bowl using a box grater. Add all the remaining filling ingredients and stir until combined. Spread on a large baking sheet and place in the oven for 20 minutes.

3 While the tofu bakes, make the enchilada sauce. Heat the olive oil in a large frying pan. Stir in the flour, smoked paprika, garlic powder, cumin, ground coriander and oregano. Whisk until smooth and cook for 1-2 minutes until very fragrant and nutty.

4 Gradually add the vegetable stock while whisking continuously, then whisk in the tomato purée, passata, sea salt and vinegar. Bring to a simmer, whisking often, then cook until thickened. Remove from the heat.

5 Spread half of the enchilada sauce over the base of a large baking dish. Remove the tofu mixture from the oven and divide between the tortillas, rolling them up tightly. Place them, seam-side down, in the dish. Pour the remaining sauce over the top and dollop the crème fraîche down the middle.

6 **If making in advance:** assemble the enchiladas as above. Allow to cool fully, then cover the dish tightly with foil or a lid and freeze for up to 3 months. When ready to bake, thaw in the fridge overnight, then preheat your oven to 220°C/Fan 200°C/Gas Mark 7 and bake as instructed below.

7 **If cooking now,** transfer the dish to the preheated oven and bake for 25 minutes, or until bubbling and golden. Serve hot, sprinkled with coriander, red onion and vegan feta.

(image on previous spread)

Serves 4

Prep time:
5 minutes

Cooking time:
10 minutes

Kale, Pistachio and Preserved Lemon Pesto Pasta

150g kale
50g shelled, roasted, unsalted pistachios, plus extra for topping
3 tbsp nutritional yeast
1 tbsp white miso paste
60ml extra-virgin olive oil, plus extra if needed
30g fresh basil, plus extra for topping
½ tsp red chilli flakes
¼ tsp ground black pepper
1 preserved lemon (or use the zest and juice of 1 lemon)
400g vegan dried pasta (such as rigatoni or penne)
Flaky sea salt

Preserved lemons have a really unique salty, tangy flavour that makes a *lot* of sense inside a bright, fresh pesto. You only use the outside of a preserved lemon, generally, so for this recipe you'll need to slice it in half and scoop out the soft flesh in the middle. Oh, and give what's left a little chop before you throw it in the food processor, just to make sure the flavour gets distributed evenly.

1 Wash the kale thoroughly, shaking off any excess water. Place the kale in a large frying pan over medium heat and cover with a lid.

2 Cook for 2 minutes, allowing the steam from the residual water to wilt the kale, stirring occasionally until just softened. Remove from the heat and let cool to room temperature.

3 Put the wilted kale in a food processor and add the pistachios, nutritional yeast, miso paste, olive oil, basil, chilli flakes and black pepper.

4 Slice the preserved lemon in half and discard the soft flesh and seeds from the middle. Roughly chop and add the rind to the food processor. Blitz until the mixture is smooth, stopping to scrape down the sides as needed.

5 Season to taste, adding salt, black pepper or a splash of olive oil, if needed to reach your desired consistency.

6 **If making ahead,** transfer the pesto to a jar and store in the fridge for up to a week.

7 **If serving now,** bring a large pot of salted water to the boil. Cook the pasta until al dente, then drain (reserving a cup of the water) and return to the pan. Stir through the pesto and loosen the sauce with a little of the reserved pasta water, if necessary.

8 Top with the extra toasted pistachios and fresh basil leaves before serving.

(image overleaf)

BALSAMIC
VINEGAR
OF MODENA

Serves 4

Prep time:
15 minutes

Cooking time:
30 minutes

Balsamic Mushroom Ragu

20g dried porcini mushrooms
150ml boiling water
1 tbsp olive oil
1 large onion, diced
3 garlic cloves, minced
1 celery stick, diced
300g chestnut mushrooms, diced as finely as you can
1 tbsp tomato purée
1 tbsp soy sauce
1 tsp vegan Worcestershire sauce
1 tsp Marmite
125ml red wine (make sure it's vegan)
2 tbsp sweet balsamic vinegar
400ml vegetable or mushroom stock
100ml passata
2 bay leaves
400g vegan dried pasta (such as pappardelle)
Ground black pepper

Can we have a moment to appreciate the chunky, glossiness of this ragu? It's got two of my favourite things in it (Marmite and mushrooms) and thus is irresistibly umami. It's important to chop the mushrooms nice and finely if you're to achieve that meaty texture, but if you're in a hurry, you can simply just use the big holes of a box grater to shred the mushrooms instead.

1 Place the dried porcini mushrooms in a small, heatproof bowl and cover them with the boiling water. Leave to rehydrate for 10 minutes.

2 Meanwhile, heat a large frying pan over medium heat and add the olive oil. Stir in the onion, garlic and celery and cook for about 5 minutes, or until the onion and garlic are browning and the celery has softened.

3 Add the mushrooms to the pan. Depending on the size of your frying pan, you may have to add the mushrooms in two batches, cooking them down between each addition.

4 Use a fork to remove the porcini mushrooms from their soaking liquid, chop them finely and add them to the pan as well, making sure to reserve the soaking liquid.

5 Cook, stirring often, for another 5 minutes until the mushrooms have softened and most of their moisture has evaporated.

6 Stir in the tomato purée, soy sauce, Worcestershire sauce, Marmite, red wine and balsamic vinegar. Simmer for a few minutes until reduced, then add the stock, passata and bay leaves. Place a fine-mesh sieve over the pan and strain in the reserved porcini soaking water.

7 Bring everything to a simmer, then cook uncovered for about 20 minutes, stirring often, or until the ragu has reduced to a thick, glossy sauce. Season with black pepper to taste, then remove the bay leaves and discard them.

(recipe continues overleaf)

8 **If making in advance,** let the ragu cool to room temperature and transfer it to an airtight container. Freeze for up to 2 months, defrosting overnight in the fridge before reheating in a saucepan over medium heat.

9 **If serving now,** cook the pasta in salted boiling water according to the package instructions. Drain, then stir in about half the ragu. Serve each portion topped with more ragu and a sprinkle of freshly ground black pepper.

Serves 4

Prep time:
15 minutes

Cooking time:
35 minutes

Smoky Squash Spaghetti

1 small butternut squash, peeled, deseeded and chopped into 2.5cm chunks
2 tbsp nutritional yeast
1 tbsp maple syrup
1 tsp smoked paprika
1 head of garlic
2 tbsp olive oil
1 tsp smoked flaky sea salt, or plain flaky sea salt
450g dried spaghetti
1 tsp Marmite
1 tbsp red miso paste
2 tbsp tomato purée
200ml vegetable stock, boiling hot
1 x 400g can cannellini beans, drained
Ground black pepper

Pretend you're the foreman of a rustic small-batch pasta sauce cannery somewhere in Tuscany and whip up a batch of this roasted squash sauce. Jar it up and keep in the fridge for Tuesday's quick-fire dinner.

1 Preheat the oven to 220°C/Fan 200°C/Gas Mark 7.

2 Toss the squash with the nutritional yeast, maple syrup and smoked paprika, then transfer to a roasting tray.

3 Slice the head of garlic in half widthways and place it in the roasting tray, sliced sides up. Drizzle with olive oil and sprinkle with smoky salt.

4 Cover the tin with foil and roast for 15 minutes, then for an additional 20 minutes uncovered, or until the squash is tender and lightly caramelised.

5 Remove from the oven and cool for 5 minutes. Squeeze the garlic cloves out of their skins onto the squash, then blitz in a blender with the Marmite, red miso paste, tomato purée, vegetable stock and cannellini beans.until smooth.

6 **If making in advance:** Transfer the blended sauce to a jar or airtight container and refrigerate for up to 3 days. Alternatively, freeze for up to 2 months.

7 **If serving straight away:** Cook the spaghetti in salted water according to the package instructions. Drain the spaghetti, reserving 250ml of the pasta water.

8 Return the spaghetti to the pan and cover it with the blended sauce. Place over low heat to warm the sauce through, stirring gently for around 2 minutes.

9 Use the reserved pasta water to thin out the sauce if it is too thick. Serve with extra black pepper on top.

(image on previous spread)

DIAL IT UP!

Top with Crispy Rosemary Pangrattato (page 240).

Serves 4

Prep time:
20 minutes

Cooking time:
35 minutes

Greens and Grains Galette

1 tbsp olive oil
1 onion, finely chopped
2 garlic cloves, minced
50g curly kale, washed and de-stemmed
50g cavolo nero, washed and de-stemmed
200g fresh spinach, washed
1 x 320g packet pre-rolled shortcrust pastry (ensure it's vegan)
½ tsp flaky sea salt
½ tsp ground black pepper
2 tbsp nutritional yeast
1 tbsp white miso paste
100g vegan cream cheese
1 tbsp Dijon mustard
1 x 250g packet microwave grains
1 tbsp unflavoured, unsweetened plant milk
1 tbsp buckwheat groats (optional)
1 tbsp sesame seeds (optional)

Here's my advice for anyone struggling to eat more greens: *wrap them in pastry!* Hand me that innovation award, baby! This galette looks (and tastes) best when thrown together with rustic abandon. Don't take too long folding it up, or the magic will be lost!

1 Line a baking sheet with baking paper and, if baking today, preheat the oven to 200°C/Fan 180°C/Gas Mark 6.

2 In a large frying pan, heat the olive oil over medium heat. Add the onion and garlic and fry until softened and fragrant, around 3-4 minutes.

3 Add the kale and cavolo nero, cooking until wilted and dark green, about 3-5 minutes. Stir in the spinach and cook until just wilted. Remove from the heat and transfer the mixture to a large plate to cool for 5-10 minutes.

4 Meanwhile unroll the shortcrust pastry onto the lined baking sheet.

5 In a large bowl, combine the slightly cooled greens mixture with the salt, pepper, nutritional yeast, miso paste, cream cheese and mustard. Break up the packet of microwave grains by squeezing it before opening, then add the grains to the bowl. Stir well until evenly combined.

6 Spoon the greens and grains mixture into a rough rectangle in the centre of the pastry, leaving a 2.5cm border on all sides. Fold the edges of the pastry over the filling, overlapping slightly to create a rustic edge.

7 Brush the pastry edges with plant milk, then sprinkle with buckwheat and sesame seeds, if using.

(recipe continues overleaf)

8 **If making in advance,** place the baking sheet in the freezer until the galette is frozen solid, about 2 hours. Once frozen, transfer to a large zip-lock bag or airtight container and return to the freezer for up to 3 months. Defrost overnight in the fridge before preheating the oven to 200°C/Fan 180°C/Gas Mark 6 and baking as below.

9 **If serving straight away,** bake the galette in the preheated oven for 30–35 minutes, or until the pastry is golden brown. Allow to cool for 5 minutes before slicing and serving.

DIAL IT UP!

Dollop with Tofu Crème Fraîche or drizzle with High-Protein Ranch Dressing (page 241) after baking and before serving.

Makes 6 large or 12 small samosas

Prep time: 20 minutes

Cooking time: 40 minutes

Muffin Tin Samosas

1 tbsp vegetable oil, plus extra for greasing and brushing
1 onion, finely chopped
2 garlic cloves, crushed
1 potato (about 200g), finely diced
250g frozen mixed vegetables (diced variety)
1 tbsp curry powder
100ml vegetable stock
2 tbsp panko breadcrumbs
10–12 large filo pastry sheets
1 tbsp nigella seeds or black sesame seeds

For the quick coriander chutney
30g fresh coriander
1 tsp ginger paste
1 green bird's eye chilli, chopped
½ tsp ground cumin
3 tbsp lemon juice
Pinch of fine sea salt

These actually look better when nice and scruffy, because when it comes to filo pastry, scruffy = ruffles! Watch the tops closely to make sure they don't burn. If they're browning too quickly, top the tray loosely with tin foil and bake until the samosa bases are crispy.

1 Lightly grease a medium 12-hole or large 6-hole muffin tin with oil and, if baking today, preheat the oven to 200°C/Fan 180°C/Gas Mark 6.

2 Heat the vegetable oil in a large frying pan over medium heat. Add the onion and garlic and cook until soft and fragrant.

3 Stir in the potato, mixed vegetables, curry powder and vegetable stock. Simmer until the vegetables are tender and most of the liquid has evaporated. Remove from heat and let cool slightly.

4 Sprinkle a pinch of panko breadcrumbs into the bottom of each muffin tin well to prevent sogginess.

5 Cut the filo pastry into squares large enough to slightly overhang the edges of the muffin tin wells (about 10–12cm). Layer three squares of filo in each well, brushing each layer with oil as you go.

6 Divide the filling evenly between the pastry-lined cups. Top with a final ruffled square of filo, brushing it with oil. Sprinkle with nigella seeds or black sesame seeds.

7 **If baking now,** transfer to the preheated oven for 25–30 minutes, or until the filo is golden and crisp and the filling is piping hot.

8 **To prepare ahead,** assemble the samosas as directed but do not bake. Freeze the samosas in the muffin tin until they are firm, then transfer them to an airtight container or freezer bag. Store for up to 3 months.

(recipe continues overleaf)

9 **To bake from frozen,** preheat the oven to 200°C/Fan 180°C/Gas Mark 6. Place the frozen samosas on a baking sheet and bake for 30–35 minutes until golden and crisp.

10 While the samosas bake, blend all the chutney ingredients until smooth, adding a tablespoon or two of water as needed to reach your preferred consistency. Taste and adjust the seasoning.

11 Serve the samosas warm with the chutney.

Serves 4

Prep time: 15 minutes

Cooking time: 40 minutes

Instant Pot Jackfruit Rendang

2 large shallots, peeled
4 large garlic cloves, peeled
1 red chilli, chopped, plus optional sliced chilli to serve
2.5cm piece of ginger, roughly sliced (no need to peel)
1 tbsp lemongrass paste
1 tbsp tamarind paste
1 tsp ground coriander
1 tbsp vegetable oil
2 x 400g cans young green jackfruit in water, drained
250g new potatoes, halved
1 tbsp light brown sugar
1 x 400ml can coconut milk
4 kaffir lime leaves
1 tbsp soy sauce
30g desiccated coconut
Juice of 1 lime

For serving
Steamed rice
Fresh coriander
Lime wedges

Let's be honest, this rendang isn't exactly the belle of the ball. Upon opening the Instant Pot, me and Becci (the incredible food stylist of this book) both had a lovely little panic attack about it. Rendang is typically made with beef, so the colour tends to be much darker and richer. But then we tasted it, and honestly, it's a contender for the most delicious recipe in this book. Mind-blowing levels of flavour that have to be tasted to be believed, and come on, who doesn't live for an ugly duckling story? If you don't have an Instant Pot or pressure cooker, don't worry! Cook in a large saucepan, then cover and simmer for an extra 15 minutes, watching closely to make sure it doesn't reduce too much.

1 Blend the shallots, garlic, chilli, ginger, lemongrass paste, tamarind paste and ground coriander to a smooth paste, adding a splash of water if needed.

2 Set the Instant Pot to Sauté mode, heat the oil, and cook the spice paste for 5 minutes until fragrant.

3 Turn off Sauté mode. Add the jackfruit, potatoes, sugar, coconut milk, lime leaves, soy sauce and 200ml water. Stir to combine.

4 Secure the lid, set the valve to Sealing, and pressure cook on High for 15 minutes. Let the pressure naturally release for 10 minutes, then manually release any remaining pressure.

5 Remove the lid and add the desiccated coconut. Cook for an extra 7-10 minutes on Sauté mode until the sauce has thickened.

6 Stir in the lime juice and fish out and discard the lime leaves.

7 **If making in advance,** transfer the rendang to four airtight containers and allow to cool fully before refrigerating for up to 4 days or freezing for up to 2 months. Defrost fully before reheating in a saucepan over medium heat.

8 Serve with steamed rice, fresh coriander and lime wedges, with extra chilli sprinkled over if you like.

Super-Quick Suppers

There comes a time in every cook's life when ambition takes a backseat to sheer, primal desperation. Maybe you had big plans - some elaborate, multi-step masterpiece that required a weekend's worth of prep and a shopping basket full of esoteric ingredients - but now? Now it's late, you're hungry, and if dinner takes longer than 25 minutes, you're fully prepared to eat dry cereal right from the box.

That's where this chapter comes in. It's a collection of meals designed for those moments when you need good vegan food and you need it *fast*. These meals come together in 25 minutes or less, with no unnecessary faff, no elaborate techniques, and absolutely no weird ingredients.

We're talking Red Curry Dumplings (page 114), ready in 13 minutes and with flavour out the wazoo! Or maybe crispy Garlic Butter Potatoes with Romesco Sauce (page 140), a dinner that's basically its own love language. Way better than a fistful of dry cereal, if you ask me...

Serves 2

Prep time:
5 minutes

Cooking time:
8 minutes

Red Curry Dumplings

1 tsp vegetable oil
2 spring onions, sliced, white and green parts separated
1½ tbsp Thai red curry paste (or yellow curry paste)
400ml vegetable stock
160ml coconut cream
2 tsp soy sauce
2 tsp brown sugar
30g frozen, shelled edamame beans
6 stems of long-stem broccoli
10 frozen vegetable gyozas
Juice of ½ lime
1 red chilli, finely sliced, to serve

Grab a bag of veggie gyozas from the freezer aisle and make the most of them with this quick one-pot wonder. Ready in 13 minutes, it's one of the fastest recipes in this book, and yet also one of the tastiest. The success of this recipe is largely determined by the curry paste you use, so make sure it's vegan and make sure it's tasty!

1 Heat the vegetable oil in a small saucepan over medium heat. Add the sliced spring onion whites and curry paste and fry for 1-2 minutes until fragrant.

2 Stir in the vegetable stock, coconut cream, soy sauce and brown sugar, stirring to combine.

3 Toss in the edamame beans and broccoli and bring the broth to a gentle simmer. Cook for 6 minutes.

4 While the broth simmers, steam the frozen gyozas using a metal sieve or bamboo steamer placed over the same small saucepan. Cover and steam according to the packet instructions until the gyozas are cooked.

5 Divide the broccoli and edamame between two bowls. Stir the lime juice into the broth, then divide between the two bowls. Arrange the steamed gyozas on top.

6 Garnish with the sliced spring onion greens and sliced chilli before serving.

Serves 4

Prep time: 5 minutes

Cooking time: 16 minutes

Kitchen Sink Fried Rice

For the sauce
3 tbsp soy sauce
1 tbsp brown sugar
2 garlic cloves, minced
1 tbsp ginger paste
1 tbsp gochujang paste
1 tsp rice vinegar
1 tsp toasted sesame oil
2 tbsp boiling water

For the fried rice
1 tbsp vegetable oil
300g extra-firm tofu, drained and cut into small cubes
120g green beans, trimmed and cut into thirds
150g red cabbage, finely shredded
1 medium carrot, peeled and cubed
100g frozen peas
400g cooked rice, cooled
3 spring onions, finely sliced
2 tbsp crushed dry roasted peanuts
Sriracha, for topping

Don't worry, you won't be frying the rice *inside* the kitchen sink. Nor will you be adding any kitchen sink to your fried rice. You will, however, be adding pretty much everything and anything to your rice (besides the kitchen sink) and frying it to golden perfection. This is one of those recipes that you can use to clear out the fridge. If you don't have the ingredients listed, but you do have other veggies which are begging to be eaten, then throw them in. You can even use a bag of mixed frozen veggies, for speed! And if you don't have any cooked rice, microwave rice pouches work perfectly too!

1 Mix all the sauce ingredients in a small bowl until the sugar dissolves, then set aside.

2 Heat the vegetable oil in a large non-stick frying pan or wok over medium-high heat. Add the tofu and cook for 4–5 minutes, or until golden on all sides.

3 Add the green beans, red cabbage, carrot and peas, and cook for 3–4 minutes, or until tender but still crisp.

4 Add the cooked rice to the pan. Stir to combine, and fry for 5 minutes, stirring occasionally to prevent sticking.

5 Pour the sauce over the rice mixture and toss well to coat evenly. Cook for another 2 minutes to heat through.

6 Stir in most of the spring onions, reserving some for garnish.

7 Serve topped with crushed peanuts, the remaining spring onions, and a drizzle of sriracha or crispy garlic chilli oil.

DIAL IT UP!

Drizzle with a little Crispy Garlic Chilli Oil (page 245) for an extra kick.

Serves 2 | Prep time: 10 minutes | Cooking time: 10 minutes

Green Bean Fritters with Whipped Tofu

150g green beans
50g spinach (fresh or frozen)
¼ tsp salt
1 tbsp ginger paste
1 tbsp garlic paste (or 2 minced garlic cloves)
1 tbsp nutritional yeast flakes
60g plain flour
30g cornflour
½ tsp baking powder
1 tbsp vegetable oil
Watercress or wild rocket, to serve

For the whipped tofu
300g firm silken tofu, drained
1 tbsp lemon juice
100g vegan feta, at room temperature

This is probably my favourite way to use up green beans that would otherwise get forgotten at the bottom of the fridge and turn into a bag of those weird worms from Ursula's cave in *The Little Mermaid*. Poor unfortunate souls! Instead, why not actually use your green beans to make these insanely bright and vibrant fritters for a light, nourishing dinner.

1 Add the green beans to a dry frying pan over high heat. Pour in 2 tablespoons water, cover with a lid and steam for 1 minute until bright green. Remove from the heat.

2 Put the spinach, salt, ginger paste, garlic paste and nutritional yeast in a food processor with 120ml water and blend until smooth.

3 In a large bowl, mix the plain flour, cornflour and baking powder. Pour in the blended liquid and stir until smooth. Add the green beans and toss to coat. Set aside while you make the whipped tofu.

4 Place the silken tofu, lemon juice and vegan feta in a food processor. Blend until whipped and fluffy. Transfer to a serving bowl and chill in the fridge.

5 Heat the vegetable oil in a large frying pan over medium heat. Scoop spoonfuls of fritter batter into the pan, ensuring they don't touch - you should have enough batter for around four fritters. Fry for 5 minutes on each side until golden and crisp.

6 Serve the fritters with the chilled whipped tofu, garnished with watercress or wild rocket.

(image on previous spread)

Serves 2

Prep time:
5 minutes

Cooking time:
20 minutes

Sticky Mango Tofu

325g extra-firm tofu, sliced into strips
2 tsp cornflour
2 tsp vegetable oil
3 tbsp mango chutney
2 tbsp soy sauce
1 tsp toasted sesame oil
1 tsp sriracha
1 tbsp ginger paste, or grated fresh ginger
1 tbsp lime juice

For serving
Boiled white rice
½ cucumber, finely sliced
Fresh coriander leaves
Lime wedges

Mango chutney is the store-cupboard superstar of this recipe, and if you ask me, it deserves a medal. The majority of the cooking time here is used to bake the tofu so that when you coat it in that tangy, spicy, sticky sauce, it'll still have a satisfying bite to it.

1 Preheat the air fryer to 180°C, or preheat the oven to 220°C/200°C Fan/Gas Mark 7.

2 Place the tofu in a bowl, sprinkle with cornflour and drizzle with vegetable oil. Cover the bowl with a plate and shake to coat the tofu evenly.

3 If air frying, transfer the tofu to the air fryer basket. If baking, transfer to a baking tray lined with baking paper. Cook for 20 minutes, shaking or flipping halfway through for even crisping.

4 Meanwhile, place a medium frying pan over medium heat. Add the mango chutney, soy sauce, toasted sesame oil, sriracha, grated ginger, lime juice and 150ml water. Bring to a simmer, then reduce the heat to low. Simmer, stirring occasionally, until the sauce is thick and sticky.

5 Remove the crispy tofu from the air fryer or oven and add it directly to the sauce in the frying pan. Stir to coat the tofu thoroughly.

6 Serve the sticky mango tofu with rice and finely sliced cucumber, topped with fresh coriander leaves and lime wedges on the side for squeezing.

(image overleaf)

Serves 2 | Prep time: 5 minutes | Cooking time: 10 minutes

Spring Veg Yaki Udon

1 tbsp vegetable oil
150g long-stem broccoli, cut into bite-sized pieces
100g sugar snap peas, trimmed
80g asparagus, trimmed and sliced
100g shelled edamame, fresh or frozen
2 x 200g packs udon noodles
2 spring onions, finely sliced

For the sauce
2 tbsp dark soy sauce
1 tbsp hoisin sauce
1 tbsp mirin
1 tsp toasted sesame oil
1 tbsp brown sugar
1 garlic clove, minced
1 tbsp ginger paste or freshly grated ginger

Ah, the perfect way to enjoy chewy udon noodles: coated in an umami-rich sauce with tender, steamed veggies. To keep your veggies fresh and crisp, keep your pan on a high heat and fry them for just a few minutes. Add a splash of water to the hot pan and cover with a lid to trap in the steam. They'll be cooked through, bright and tender in no time.

1 In a small bowl, whisk together all the sauce ingredients.

2 Heat the vegetable oil in a wok or large frying pan over medium-high heat. Stir-fry the veggies for 2-3 minutes, until just tender.

3 Add the udon noodles and a small splash of water to help them soften. Cover with a lid and steam for 3 minutes. Gently break the noodles apart with a spatula and stir to combine with the veggies.

4 Pour in the sauce, toss everything to coat evenly, and cook for a further 1-2 minutes.

5 Top with spring onions, divide between two bowls and serve hot.

Serves 2

Prep time: 5 minutes

Cooking time: 15 minutes

Sardinian Herby Fregola Soup

2 tsp olive oil
1 small onion, finely diced
2 garlic cloves, finely sliced
¼ tsp chilli flakes
½ tsp fennel seeds
¼ tsp ground black pepper
50g fresh fennel, finely sliced
100ml white wine
800ml vegetable stock
100g fregola (or use any small pasta, Israeli couscous or orzo)
Pinch of flaky sea salt
100g drained canned butter beans, or cannellini beans
4 stems cavolo nero, or curly kale, destemmed and roughly chopped
2 tbsp nutritional yeast
1 tbsp lemon juice
Small bunch of fresh dill, finely chopped
Small bunch of fresh chives, finely chopped
Small bunch of fresh basil, finely chopped

As founder and treasurer of the fregola fan club, 'Friends of Fregola', I take any opportunity to tell people about the underrated majesty of my favourite tiny pasta (or massive couscous, depending on how you look at it). Just yesterday I had a wonderful one-sided conversation about fregola with the guy who came to check the gas meter, or maybe he was robbing my silverware... anyway, what matters is that he was really interested in fregola. It works perfectly in this recipe because it cooks in a flash and helps to thicken the broth at the same time. It adds a nice bite to the soup too, and if you can find the hand-made stuff that's various different shades of brown, it'll taste different in every mouthful.

1. Heat the oil in a saucepan and fry the onion, garlic, chilli flakes, fennel seeds and fennel until browning. Deglaze the pan with the white wine and cook for a minute to reduce.
2. Add the vegetable stock, fregola and salt and bring to the boil. Cover and cook for 10 minutes, or until the fregola is tender.
3. Add the drained butter beans and cavolo nero. Simmer for 2 minutes.
4. Remove from the heat and stir in the nutritional yeast and lemon juice. Top with herbs and serve.

Serves 2

Prep time:
5 minutes

Cooking time:
10 minutes

Quick Kimchi Biang Biang Noodles

200g pack fresh flat, wheat noodles (I use the Itsu brand)
3 tbsp vegetable oil
2 spring onions, roughly chopped
1 tsp Szechuan peppercorns, crushed
2 garlic cloves, finely sliced
2 tsp chilli flakes (use a mild variety, such as Korean gochugaru or Aleppo)
50g vegan kimchi, drained and roughly chopped
2 tbsp Chinese black vinegar or balsamic vinegar
2 tbsp soy sauce
½ cucumber, julienned, to serve
Small bunch of fresh coriander, roughly torn, to serve

For this recipe, I like to use the flat, wheat noodles that look like frilly white ribbons. They're the closest to actual biang biang noodles, which are a kind of Chinese hand-stretched noodle, named after the sound they make as they slap the surface of the table. The sweet acidity of Chinese black vinegar is key to the piquancy of the sauce, so it's worth getting your hands on a bottle if you can. In a pinch, balsamic vinegar will work as a substitute.

1 Place a small saucepan of water over medium heat and bring to the boil. Cook the noodles according to the package instructions.

2 While the noodles cook, heat the vegetable oil in a small frying pan until very hot. Add the spring onions, Szechuan peppercorns, garlic and chilli flakes all at once, then immediately turn off the heat.

3 Drain the cooked noodles and return them to the saucepan. Add the kimchi, black rice vinegar, soy sauce and the chilli oil in the frying pan. Gently stir to coat the noodles evenly.

4 Divide the noodles between two bowls and top with the julienned cucumber and torn coriander. Serve immediately.

Serves 2

Prep time:
10 minutes

Cooking time:
25 minutes

Crispy Rice Satay Salad

250g leftover jasmine rice (or a 250g pouch microwave jasmine rice, or any cooked white rice)
60g curly kale
1 tsp olive oil
Pinch of sea salt
1 hass avocado, peeled, pitted and sliced
150g cooked edamame beans
½ cucumber, sliced
50g dry roasted peanuts, roughly chopped
10g fresh mint, finely chopped
10g fresh coriander, finely chopped
1 red chilli, deseeded and finely sliced
1 spring onion, finely sliced

For the satay dressing
2 tbsp chunky peanut butter
Juice of 2 limes
1 garlic clove, finely minced or grated
1 tsp ginger paste
2 tbsp soy sauce
1 tsp toasted sesame oil
2 tsp maple syrup
1 tbsp sriracha

Two friends came for dinner the other day and, in true 'me' fashion, I ended up cooking about 10kg of rice, as a side dish. I could blame the excess on my dyscalculia, or perhaps my measuring cups are too large, but in truth, I just really wanted to make this salad the next day. It's nutty and toasty with loads of fresh herbs and a kick of chilli. But the star of the show is that crispy baked rice. It's like stirring hundreds of perfect tiny croûtons through your salad, so every bite is jaw rattlingly satisfying.

1 Preheat the oven to 220°C/200°C Fan/Gas Mark 7.

2 Spread out the rice evenly on a baking tray lined with baking paper. Bake for 25 minutes or until crispy, stirring halfway through for even crispiness.

3 While the rice bakes, prepare the kale. Put it in a large salad bowl and massage with the olive oil and a pinch of salt for about 2 minutes until softened.

4 To the same bowl add the avocado, edamame beans, cucumber, peanuts, mint, coriander, red chilli and spring onions.

5 To make the satay dressing, whisk together the ingredients in a small bowl until smooth.

6 When the rice is crisp and golden, remove it from the oven and allow it to cool slightly. Add the crispy rice to the salad bowl.

7 Drizzle the satay dressing over the salad and serve immediately.

Serves 2

Prep time:
5 minutes

Cooking time:
20 minutes

Roasted Tomato and Tamarind Dal

100g dried split red lentils
200g store-bought slow-roasted tomatoes in oil (or sun-dried tomatoes), finely chopped
2 shallots, finely diced
2 garlic cloves, sliced
1 tsp ginger paste
1 tsp ground turmeric
2 tsp garam masala
1 tsp Kashmiri chilli powder (or any mild chilli powder)
2 tbsp tomato purée
750ml boiling water
2 tsp tamarind paste
½ tsp fine sea salt

For serving
2 tbsp vegan coconut yoghurt
Fresh coriander
Roti, rice or naan

Nobody's got time to roast tomatoes for dinner these days. We've all got somewhere to be! In fact, I'm running out the door right now to catch the last 20 minutes of my dog's flute recital. Luckily, I had half an hour to spare and a packet of those slow-roasted tomatoes from the tapas section of my local supermarket. They make this dal taste like it's been simmering for hours, which couldn't be further from the truth.

1 Rinse the lentils thoroughly in a sieve under cold running water.

2 Heat a medium saucepan over medium heat and add 1 tablespoon of the oil from the roasted tomatoes. Fry the shallots, garlic and ginger paste for 2 minutes until fragrant.

3 Stir in the turmeric, garam masala and chilli powder, followed by the tomato purée and the chopped roasted tomatoes.

4 Add the boiling water, tamarind paste, rinsed lentils and salt. Stir, bring the mixture to a boil, then lower the heat and simmer for 15 minutes, stirring occasionally, until the lentils are cooked but retain some texture.

5 Divide between two bowls and serve hot, topped with a dollop of vegan coconut yoghurt, some fresh coriander and cooked rice or naan on the side.

Serves 4

Prep time:
10 minutes

Cooking time:
10 minutes

Quick Chickpea Kati Rolls

For the chickpea filling
1 tsp olive oil
1 small onion, chopped
2 garlic cloves, minced
½ tsp mild chilli powder
1 tbsp garam masala
½ tsp salt
2 tbsp tomato purée
2 tsp brown sugar
1 red pepper, deseeded and sliced
1 x 400g can chickpeas, drained and rinsed

For serving
4 large parathas or rotis
1 small red onion, sliced
1 cucumber, finely sliced
Coriander, roughly chopped
100g unflavoured, unsweetened vegan yoghurt
1 lemon, chopped into wedges

Back when I was a street-food vendor in London, I used to trade food with other stalls to keep lunch interesting. The kati rolls from my friends at 'Kolkati' were one of the highlights. Flaky parathas stuffed with sweet and spicy fillings, packed with sharp pickled onions and bright, fresh herbs. This recipe is a vegan riff on those rolls,

1 Heat a frying pan over medium heat and add the olive oil. Add the onion and garlic and fry for 2-3 minutes. Add the chilli powder, garam masala, salt, tomato purée, brown sugar and 100ml water. Bring to a simmer and cook for another 2-3 minutes, or until the sauce has reduced to a thick paste.

2 Add the red pepper and chickpeas and cook for 5 minutes more, stirring regularly to coat the chickpeas with the sauce.

3 While the chickpeas cook, fry the parathas according to the package instructions or warm the wraps for a few seconds in the microwave.

4 Spread some yoghurt on each roti or paratha, then top with sliced red onion and cucumber and fresh coriander. Divide the cooked chickpeas between the wraps or parathas and squeeze over the lemon wedges. Fold or roll and serve warm, or if needed, wrap in foil or baking paper for a grab-and-go meal.

DIAL IT UP!

Brighten things up by switching the sliced red onion for Pink Pickled Onions (page 246).

Serves 4

Prep time:
5 minutes

Cooking time:
20 minutes

Potato and Broad Bean Chowder

1 tbsp olive oil
1 small onion, finely chopped
2 garlic cloves, minced
1 tsp tomato purée
Pinch of cayenne pepper
125ml vegan dry white wine
450g new potatoes, cut into chunks
1.5 litres vegetable stock
150g frozen broad beans
10g fresh dill, roughly chopped
200ml vegan crème fraîche (page 241 or shop-bought), or unflavoured, unsweetened vegan yoghurt
Sea salt and ground black pepper
Pinch of smoked paprika, to serve

For convenience here, I'm recommending you use frozen broad beans, but if you have access to fresh ones and they're in season, then definitely use those instead. Oh, and heads up, some brands of vegan yoghurt might split when adding them to the hot broth. To avoid this, take a ladle and half-fill it with broth. Stir the yoghurt into the ladle, rather than the entire pan of chowder, then slowly stir into the pan.

1 Heat the olive oil in a large saucepan over medium heat. Add the onion and garlic and cook for 2–3 minutes until softening and starting to brown. Stir in the tomato purée and cayenne pepper.

2 Pour in the white wine, stirring to deglaze the pan, and simmer for 1 minute to reduce slightly.

3 Add the potato chunks and vegetable stock. Bring to a boil, then reduce to a simmer. Cook for 10 minutes, or until the potatoes are tender.

4 Stir in the frozen broad beans and half of the fresh dill and cook for an additional 2–4 minutes, or until the beans are warmed through.

5 Remove from the heat and stir in the vegan crème fraîche. Season with salt.

6 Serve hot, garnished with fresh dill and a sprinkle of freshly ground black pepper and smoked paprika.

Serves 2

Prep time:
5 minutes

Cooking time:
20 minutes

One-Pot Gochujang Pasta with Chive Oil

1 tbsp vegetable oil
1 onion finely chopped
3 garlic cloves, minced
2 tbsp gochujang
1 tablespoon tomato purée
600ml boiling water
1 vegetable stock cube
300g vegan dried pasta (such as radiatori or fusilli)
150g unflavoured, unsweetened vegan yoghurt, or Tofu Crème Fraîche (page 241)

For the chive oil
10g fresh chives, roughly chopped, plus optional extra to serve
3 tbsp extra-virgin olive oil
Pinch of flaky sea salt

Gochujang is so wonderful because it's not just any old hot sauce. Since it's fermented, it brings so much more flavour and sweetness and smokiness to the table. That's why this recipe works with so few ingredients - because gochujang is such a powerhouse. And yes, I know 300g of pasta feels like a lot for two people, but taste it first and thank me later.

1 Heat the vegetable oil in a large, deep saucepan over medium heat. Add the onion and cook, stirring frequently, until soft and translucent. Add the garlic and cook for another minute.

2 Stir in the gochujang and tomato purée and cook for 2 minutes to release their flavours. Add the boiling water and crumble in the vegetable stock cube, stirring until dissolved.

3 Add the pasta to the pan, ensuring it's submerged in the liquid. Reduce the heat to low, cover the pan with a lid, and cook for 10–12 minutes, stirring occasionally, until the pasta is al dente and the sauce has thickened.

4 While the pasta cooks, prepare the chive oil. Put the chives, olive oil and salt in a mortar and pestle. Grind until the oil is rough and bright green. If you don't have a mortar and pestle, roughly chop everything together and stir in the olive oil in a small bowl.

5 Once the pasta is cooked, stir in the vegan yoghurt or tofu crème fraîche. Mix until well combined, adjusting the seasoning if needed.

6 Serve the pasta topped with spoonfuls of the chive oil. Garnish with extra chives if desired.

Serves 2

Prep time: 15 minutes

Cooking time: 25 minutes

Garlic Butter Potatoes with Romesco Sauce

For the potatoes

600g new potatoes, sliced into 2cm chunks
1 tbsp olive oil
20g vegan butter, melted
2 garlic cloves, finely minced
1 tbsp fresh chives, finely chopped
¼ tsp flaky sea salt

For the romesco sauce

75g sun-dried tomatoes (about 5-6 tomatoes)
1 x 450g jar roasted red peppers, drained
1 garlic clove, crushed
1 tbsp red wine vinegar
1 tsp smoked paprika
½ tsp fine sea salt
2 tbsp natural almond butter
200g firm tofu, drained

After eight years of marriage, I've come to learn that my love language is potatoes. Not just any potatoes, though. *These* potatoes. Golden and crispy and tossed in vegan garlic butter, then served on silky, smoky romesco sauce. Luckily, they only take 20 minutes to make, so I can still technically claim to be low maintenance. But head's up, this recipe works best with leftover boiled potatoes that have been cooked and allowed to cool. You'll get a much crispier potato this way. If using pre-cooked spuds, reduce the air-frying time by 10 minutes.

1. Preheat your air fryer to 200°C or oven to 220°C/200°C Fan/Gas Mark 7.
2. Place the new potatoes in a large bowl. Drizzle with the olive oil and toss to coat evenly.
3. Transfer to the air fryer basket and cook for 20 minutes, shaking the basket halfway through cooking. If baking, transfer to a baking sheet and bake for 25 minutes or until golden and crispy.
4. While the potatoes cook, prepare the garlic butter by stirring together the melted vegan butter, garlic, chives and salt. Set aside.
5. To make the romesco sauce, blend together the ingredients until smooth.
6. When the potatoes are cooked, transfer them to a large bowl. Pour over the garlic butter and toss to coat.
7. To serve, spread a generous layer of romesco sauce on two plates. Top with the crispy potatoes and serve immediately.

DIAL IT UP!

For extra texture, sprinkle with Crispy Rosemary Pangrattato (page 240) right before serving.

Toss the potatoes in Crispy Garlic Chilli Oil (page 245) instead of the vegan garlic butter for a spicy twist.

Serves 4

Prep time: 10 minutes

Cooking time: 5 minutes

Mexican Street Corn Salad with Lime Crema Dressing

For the salad
1 x 325g can sweetcorn, drained
2 shallots, finely chopped
1 red pepper, deseeded and cubed
1 x 400g can black beans, drained and rinsed
30g fresh coriander, roughly chopped
1 large avocado, peeled, pitted and cubed
200g vegan feta cheese, drained and crumbled
200g cherry tomatoes, halved

For the lime crema dressing
50ml unflavoured, unsweetened vegan yoghurt
60ml vegan mayonnaise
1 garlic clove, minced
Zest and juice of 1 lime
2 tsp agave syrup
½ tsp fine sea salt
½ tsp smoked paprika
¼ tsp chipotle chilli powder, plus optional extra to serve

For this recipe, we char some sweetcorn in a dry pan to mimic the smoky/sweet flavour of a Mexican grilled corn-on-the-cob snack called *'elotes'*. I did a vegan take on *elotes* in my first book, which is definitely worth a try, but this recipe literally makes more of a meal out of it. It's a jam-packed salad that works equally well as a main or a side.

1 Place a large, dry frying pan over the highest heat.

2 Once very hot, add the drained sweetcorn and toast for 2 minutes, or until lightly charred. Immediately remove from the pan and add to a large salad bowl. Add the remaining salad ingredients.

3 In a small bowl, whisk together the lime crema dressing ingredients.

4 Pour the crema over the salad and toss together. Before serving, sprinkle with a little extra chipotle chilli powder, if desired.

DIAL IT UP!

Add some toasty spice with a bit of Cheat's Salsa Macha (page 245).

Family Feasts

There's a special kind of chaos that comes with feeding a group. Whether it's your family, a pack of hungry friends, or just you and a suspiciously large appetite you refuse to explain, cooking a *lot* of food in a short amount of time is tricky.

But fear not! This chapter is here to arm you with meals that are quick, delicious and actually feed four or more people. These are the recipes you pull out when you need something impressive but fuss-free - the kind of food that makes everyone go quiet for the first few bites (a rare and glorious moment in any gathering). They're easy enough for school nights, special enough for a proper sit-down meal and - perhaps most importantly - designed to avoid relying on an emergency toast course.

From my Harissa Cauliflower Pilaf (page 165), that's an entire meal in one pot, to my Roasted Squash Fajitas with Hot Chocolate Black Beans (page 151), I've got your back. So, whether you're feeding your actual family, your chosen family, or just a table full of people who somehow all arrived *exactly* at dinnertime, these recipes will keep everyone happy, full, and - most importantly - out of the kitchen while you cook.

Serves 4

Prep time:
10 minutes

Cooking time:
20 minutes

Mushroom Lomo Saltado

500g frozen thin-cut fries
½ tsp fine sea salt
1 tbsp olive oil
4 large Portobello mushrooms, sliced into thick strips
2 red onions, sliced into wedges
2 red peppers, deseeded and sliced into strips
3 garlic cloves, minced
2 tbsp soy sauce
1 tbsp red wine vinegar
1 tbsp maple syrup
½ tsp ground black pepper
2 large tomatoes, cut into wedges
Handful of fresh coriander, chopped
Steamed white rice, to serve

I was asked to describe this recipe by my husband the other day, who was about to get it for dinner. It has a fascinating, complicated history that involves the assimilation of Chinese cooking techniques into Peruvian cuisine as a result of the international slave trade. I was about seven minutes into my ethno-gastronomic monologue deep-dive when I heard husband's stomach growl and realised that he had involuntarily zoned out due to hunger. 'It's French fry stir fry' I said, and handed him the plate.

1 Preheat the oven to 220°C/Fan 200°C/Gas Mark 7, or air fryer to 200°C. Spread the frozen fries in a single layer on a baking sheet or in the air fryer basket and cook for 15–18 minutes, shaking halfway through, until golden and crispy. Season with the fine sea salt.

2 Meanwhile, heat the olive oil in a large pan or wok over medium-high heat. Add the mushrooms and cook for 5 minutes until browned.

3 Add the red onions and red peppers and stir-fry for 3–4 minutes until slightly softened. Stir in the garlic, soy sauce, red wine vinegar, maple syrup and black pepper. Cook for another 2 minutes.

4 Gently fold in the tomato wedges and cook for 1 minute, until just softened but still holding their shape.

5 Add the crispy fries to the pan and toss gently to coat in the sauce. Sprinkle with fresh coriander and serve immediately with steamed white rice.

Serves 4

Prep time:
10 minutes

Cooking time:
35 minutes

Cauliflower Cheese Pasta Bake

1 head cauliflower (around 650g), broken into small florets
300g dried conchiglie pasta
480ml unflavoured, unsweetened plant milk
2 tbsp white miso paste
4 tbsp nutritional yeast
1 tsp English mustard
1 tsp garlic powder
1 tsp onion powder
1 tsp fine sea salt
¼ tsp ground black pepper
2 tbsp olive oil
3 tbsp plain flour

Life as an adult is all about balance, and therefore for dinner today I've chosen to balance a vegetable (cauliflower) with lots of pasta, in a very adult way. I mean, why not? It's a fantastic hybrid of two 80s school-night dinner classics: cauliflower cheese and pasta bake. Oh, and I hate to break it to you, but if you remember the 80s, then you're most certainly adult enough for this dinner.

1 Preheat your oven to 220°C/Fan 200°C/Gas Mark 7.

2 Bring a medium saucepan of salted water to a boil. Add the cauliflower florets, any of the smaller cauliflower leaves, and pasta. Boil for 5 minutes. Drain and transfer to an oven dish.

3 In a measuring jug, blend together the plant milk, miso paste, mustard, nutritional yeast, garlic powder, onion powder, salt, and black pepper with an immersion blender.

4 Place a saucepan over medium heat and add the olive oil. Once hot, whisk in the flour to form a roux. Allow it to bubble away for 2 minutes until the roux browns very slightly. Gradually pour in the plant milk mixture, whisking continuously, until you have a thick, glossy béchamel-style sauce.

5 Remove the sauce from the heat and pour it over the pasta and cauliflower. Stir gently to coat everything evenly.

6 Bake in the preheated oven for 25 minutes or until golden brown on top. Allow to cool for a few minutes before serving.

(image on previous spread)

Serves 4

Prep time:
10 minutes

Cooking time:
30 minutes

Roasted Squash Fajitas with Hot Chocolate Black Beans

1 butternut squash, peeled, deseeded and sliced
1 large red onion, peeled and sliced
1 red pepper, deseeded and sliced
1 tsp ground cumin
1 tsp mild chilli powder
1 tsp dried oregano
½ tsp garlic powder
1 tbsp smoked paprika
2 tbsp light brown sugar
1 tsp flaky sea salt
½ tsp ground black pepper
2 tbsp olive oil

For the hot chocolate black beans
1 x 400g can black beans
1 vegetable stock cube
½ tsp chilli powder
1 tbsp soy sauce
1 tbsp tomato purée
45g dark chocolate, chopped into chunks

For serving
1 avocado, mashed
Juice of a fresh lime, plus more lime wedges
8 flour tortillas
Fresh coriander
Sliced red chilli (optional)

I've been putting dark chocolate in chilli for a while now and it's a game changer, but these black beans are something else. They're inspired by Mexican mole sauce, and because they're baked in their own starchy soaking liquid, they end up rich and creamy every time. Paired with sweet and spicy roasted squash and tangy lime-spiked avocado, it's a match made in fajita heaven.

1 Preheat the oven to 220°C/Fan 200°C/Gas Mark 7.

2 Place the squash, red onion and red pepper in a large bowl. Add the cumin, chilli powder, oregano, garlic powder, smoked paprika, brown sugar, sea salt, black pepper and olive oil. Toss to coat well, then spread the mixture on a large baking sheet. Set aside.

3 Put the black beans (including the liquid in the can), vegetable stock cube, chilli powder, soy sauce, tomato purée and dark chocolate in an oven-safe saucepan.

4 Set over medium heat and cook just until the beans start to bubble. Remove from the heat and transfer to the oven. At the same time, place the tray of squash and vegetables in the oven, on a separate shelf. Roast both for 30 minutes, stirring the vegetables halfway through.

5 Meanwhile, mix the mashed avocado with the lime juice in a small bowl.

6 Remove the roasted vegetables and beans from the oven.

7 To serve, load up tortillas with black beans, roasted vegetables and squash, mashed avocado, fresh coriander and red chillies, if you want things hotter. Serve with extra lime wedges on the side.

(image overleaf)

Serves 4-6

Prep time:
10 minutes

Cooking time:
30 minutes

Caramelised Jalapeño Chilli

1 tbsp olive oil
1 onion, finely chopped
2 garlic cloves, minced
85g fresh jalapeños, deseeded and roughly chopped (or use pickled if you can't find fresh)
2 tbsp brown sugar
2 tbsp white wine vinegar
1 x 400g can red kidney beans, drained and rinsed
1 x 400g can pinto beans, drained and rinsed
1 x 400g can black beans, drained and rinsed
500ml passata
1 red pepper, deseeded and cubed
1 tbsp ground cumin
2 tsp dried oregano
1 bay leaf
1 tbsp cocoa powder
1 tbsp dark soy sauce
300ml boiling vegetable stock

For serving
Steamed rice or jacket potatoes
Fresh chives, finely chopped
Salted tortilla chips, for dipping

I told my friend Kelly that I needed a chilli recipe for this book but that I was struggling to make it unique, without overcomplicating things. Her eyes lit up immediately and I knew she had a great idea. It was Kelly's idea to caramelise fresh jalapeños at the very start of the recipe, almost like you're making a chutney, and I think she deserves a James Beard award for 'Best Supporting Friend of a Cookbook Author'. Eighty-five grams of jalapeños feels like a lot for a chilli, I know, but once caramelised, the sweetness mellows out the heat without losing any of their fruitiness. It's a true chilli revelation.

1 Heat the olive oil in a large saucepan over medium heat. Add the onion, garlic and jalapeños and fry for 5 minutes until softened. Stir in the brown sugar and white wine vinegar and cook for a further 2 minutes until caramelised. Be careful not to breathe in the steam - it'll make you cough.

2 Add the remaining ingredients and bring to a simmer, then cover and cook for 20 minutes, stirring occasionally. Remove the bay leaf before serving.

3 Serve with steamed rice and tortilla chips or jacket potatoes, topped with fresh chives.

DIAL IT UP!

Take the edge off the heat with a swirl of Tofu Crème Fraîche (page 241).

Serves 4

Prep time:
10 minutes

Cooking time:
40 minutes

Dukkah-Crusted Aubergines

1 red pepper, deseeded and sliced
1 x 400g can chickpeas, drained
140g green olives, pitted
300g cherry tomatoes
200g unflavoured, unsweetened vegan yoghurt
Zest and juice of 1 lemon
3 tbsp harissa paste
1 tbsp maple syrup or agave syrup
2 garlic cloves, minced
1 tsp fine sea salt
2 aubergines, cut in half lengthways
1 tbsp olive oil
Fresh coriander sprigs, to serve (optional)
Couscous or flatbreads, to serve

For the dukkah
80g unsalted nuts, finely chopped (almonds, hazelnuts, pistachios, walnuts, or a mix)
1 tsp cumin seeds
1 tsp coriander seeds
1 tsp ground cumin
1 tsp ground coriander
1 tsp white sesame seeds
1 tsp flaky sea salt

Next time you're faced with an awkward silence in a conversation, my tip is to ask 'In your opinion, what's the most pointless vegetable?' It's my favourite ice breaker, ideal for when you find yourself erroneously placed on the boring table at a wedding or awkwardly waiting for a zoom meeting to start. And I'm sorry to say that the most common answer I come across is aubergine! Personally, I couldn't agree less, so this recipe is deliberately designed to showcase the magic of aubergines - twice roasted and coated with toasted nuts and spices. You'll grow to love this vegetable, which most definitely has a point (although not literally, they're actually very round).

1 Preheat the oven to 200°C/Fan 180°C/Gas Mark 6.

2 Put the red pepper, chickpeas, olives and cherry tomatoes in a roasting tray.

3 In a bowl, mix the yoghurt, lemon zest and juice, harissa, maple syrup, garlic and fine sea salt. Spoon half over the vegetables and stir to coat.

4 Rub the aubergine halves with olive oil and place them in the tray, cut sides up. Cover the tray with foil and roast for 30 minutes.

5 Meanwhile, make the dukkah. Toast the nuts, coriander seeds and cumin seeds in a dry frying pan until golden (about 2-3 minutes), being careful not to let them burn. Transfer to a bowl and mix with the ground spices, sesame seeds and flaky salt.

6 Remove the foil from the tray and spoon the remaining yoghurt mixture over the tops of the aubergines, spreading it right to the edges. Sprinkle with the dukkah and return to the oven for another 10 minutes.

7 Sprinkle with coriander, if using, and serve with couscous or flatbreads.

Makes
9 sliders

Prep time:
15 minutes

Cooking time:
30 minutes

BBQ Jackfruit Sliders with Ranch Slaw

2 x 400g cans young green jackfruit, drained
2 tsp garlic powder
1 tbsp smoked paprika
2 tsp ground cumin
½ tsp cayenne pepper
120g ketchup
2 tbsp dark soy sauce
3 tbsp maple syrup
2 tbsp white wine vinegar
2 tbsp olive oil
20g vegan butter, melted
9 small burger buns

For the ranch slaw
200g sweetheart cabbage, shredded
2 spring onions, sliced
1 celery stick, sliced
10g fresh parsley, finely chopped
10g fresh dill, finely chopped
10g fresh chives, finely chopped
1 garlic clove, grated
100g vegan yoghurt
100g vegan mayonnaise
1 tbsp white wine vinegar
Sea salt and ground black pepper

These sliders make for great party food because they require no pre-cooking, so you can assemble them in advance and just throw them in the oven as people arrive. In fact, I currently have a batch in the oven for my dog's surprise toga party. It's a surprise because she's a dog and doesn't know what a toga is. Oh but, heads up, these sliders are deliciously messy, so you'll need a few napkins if you value the whiteness of your toga.

1 Preheat the oven to 220°C/Fan 200°C/Gas Mark 7.

2 In a bowl, shred the jackfruit with a fork. Mix with the garlic powder, smoked paprika, cumin, cayenne, ketchup, soy sauce, maple syrup, white wine vinegar and olive oil.

3 Brush a roasting tin with half of the melted vegan butter. Slice the burger buns in half and arrange the bottom halves in the tin.

4 Spoon the BBQ jackfruit onto the buns, then place the top halves back on. Brush the tops with the remaining melted vegan butter.

5 Cover the roasting tin tightly with foil and bake for 20 minutes. Remove the foil and bake for a further 10 minutes.

6 Meanwhile, mix together the cabbage, spring onions, celery, parsley, dill, chives, garlic, yoghurt, mayonnaise and white wine vinegar. Season with salt and pepper to taste.

7 To serve, lift the tops off the buns and add a generous spoonful of ranch slaw to each slider before replacing the lids.

DIAL IT UP!

Serve with High-Protein Ranch Dressing (page 241) or Quick Ketchup (page 242) on the side, for dunking.

Serves 6

Prep time:
10 minutes

Cooking time:
25 minutes

Leftover Pasta Frittata

200g passata
1 tbsp tomato purée
2 tbsp gram flour (chickpea flour)
2 tbsp cornflour
1 tsp fine sea salt
½ tsp garlic powder
2 tbsp olive oil
250g leftover cooked pasta (spaghetti works best)
100ml hot water (optional)
100g sun-dried tomatoes, roughly chopped
140g chargrilled artichoke hearts, roughly chopped
150g cherry tomatoes, halved
50g vegan feta, crumbled
Small bunch of fresh parsley or basil, roughly chopped
Side salad, to serve (optional)

Use up last night's leftovers in this pasta-bake/frittata hybrid. I've used my favourite antipasti veggies - like sun-dried tomatoes, artichoke hearts and roasted red peppers - but feel free to sub these with your favourite antipasti.

1 Preheat the oven to 220°C/Fan 200°C/Gas Mark 7.

2 Blend the passata, tomato purée, gram flour, cornflour, sea salt, garlic powder, and 1 tablespoon of the olive oil in a blender until very smooth.

3 Heat a medium oven-safe frying pan over medium heat and add the remaining 1 tablespoon olive oil. Once hot, add the leftover pasta to the pan. If the pasta is clumped together, add a splash of hot water to loosen it.

4 Stir the sun-dried tomatoes and artichoke hearts into the pasta. Pour the blended mixture over the pasta, jiggling the pan slightly to ensure everything is evenly coated - do not stir.

5 Top with the halved cherry tomatoes, followed by the crumbled vegan feta. Cook over medium heat for 5 minutes. Transfer the pan to the preheated oven and bake for 20 minutes, or until the frittata has set and is golden brown on top.

6 Slice and top with the fresh herbs, then serve hot with a side salad. Alternatively, allow the frittata to cool to room temperature, slice, then refrigerate for up to 3 days. Serve reheated or cold.

Serves 4

Prep time:
10 minutes

Cooking time:
20 minutes

Loaded Gyros Fries

800g frozen French fries
450g extra-firm tofu, drained
1 tbsp olive oil
1 tsp garlic powder
1 tsp ground cumin
1 tsp paprika
½ tsp dried oregano
1 tsp dark soy sauce
1 white pita bread
1 tbsp Magic Roast Chicken Salt (page 244)
1 large red onion, finely sliced
½ cucumber, sliced
200g cherry tomatoes, halved
100g vegan feta, crumbled

For the yoghurt dressing
100g vegan yoghurt
1 small garlic clove, minced
1 tbsp extra-virgin olive oil
10g fresh dill, plus more for topping
Juice and zest of 1 lemon
Sea salt and ground black pepper

A few years ago, I was lucky enough to host a group vacation to Greece with the amazing vegan travel company, The Getaway Co. We ate a *lot* of memorable food on that trip, but chief among them were the vegan gyros we had in Athens. Think crispy golden fries with shaved, marinated tofu in a soft pita with fresh salad and tzatziki. This recipe is my attempt to turn those gyros into something big and shareable that'll feed the whole family.

1 Preheat the oven to 220°C/Fan 200°C/Gas Mark 7. Spread the fries on a baking tray.

2 Slice the tofu as thinly as you can, then place it in a bowl. Add ½ tbsp of the olive oil, the garlic powder, cumin, paprika, dried oregano and dark soy sauce. Mix carefully until coated, trying not to break up the tofu too much. Spread over half of a separate baking tray.

3 Slice the pita into strips and place them in the same bowl. Toss with the remaining ½ tablespoon olive oil, then spread on the empty half of the second baking tray.

4 Place the fries in the oven and bake for 20 minutes. After 10 minutes, place the tofu and pita tray in the oven to bake for the remaining 10 minutes.

5 To make the yoghurt dressing, whisk together the vegan yoghurt, garlic, extra-virgin olive oil, dill, lemon juice and lemon zest in a small bowl. Season with salt and pepper to taste, then set aside.

6 Remove both trays from the oven. Sprinkle the fries with magic roast chicken salt. Top with the tofu and pita, followed by the red onion, cucumber, cherry tomatoes and crumbled vegan feta. Drizzle with the yoghurt dressing, then top with fresh dill right before serving.

Serves 4

Prep time:
10 minutes

Cooking time:
25 minutes

Harissa Cauliflower Pilaf with Quick Chermoula

250g white basmati rice
500ml vegetable stock, boiling hot
1 tbsp tomato purée
2 tbsp harissa paste
1 x 400g can chickpeas, drained
250g cauliflower florets
20g roasted, unsalted almonds, roughly chopped, to serve

For the chermoula
10g fresh parsley
10g fresh coriander
1 garlic clove, roughly crushed
2 tsp pomegranate molasses
Juice of 1 lemon
2 tbsp extra-virgin olive oil
1 tsp za'atar
½ tsp chilli flakes (I use Aleppo chilli flakes)
½ tsp fine sea salt

Is there anything more satisfying than pulling perfectly cooked rice out of the oven? I guess maybe a hot stone massage, or an ASMR sound bath, but who's indulging in either of those on a Tuesday night? This is a complete meal in one pan and the recipe is almost entirely hands free. It's somehow both simple enough to make for a busy school-night dinner and yet impressive enough to serve to guests.

1 Preheat your oven to 220°C/Fan 200°C/Gas Mark 7. Wash the rice in a medium bowl and drain through a sieve.

2 Place the rice in an ovenproof pan. Add the stock, tomato purée and harissa paste. Stir to break up the tomato purée and harissa, then place over medium heat.

3 As soon as the pot starts to simmer, remove from the heat and top with the chickpeas and cauliflower florets. Cover the pot with a lid or tightly with foil.

4 Bake in the preheated oven for 15 minutes.

5 Meanwhile, blend together all the ingredients for the chermoula. (If you don't have a blender, finely chop the herbs and mince the garlic, then stir together in a small bowl with the remaining ingredients.)

6 After 15 minutes, remove the lid or foil from the pan and bake uncovered for an additional 10 minutes.

7 Remove from the oven. Drizzle the chermoula over the rice and sprinkle with the roasted almonds before serving.

Serves 4

Prep time: 20 minutes

Cooking time: 20 minutes

Maple Mustard Pretzel Crusted Tofu Sandwiches with Broccoli Slaw

For the pretzel-crusted tofu
450g extra-firm tofu
1 tsp fine sea salt
2 tbsp Dijon mustard
2 tsp wholegrain mustard
2 tbsp maple syrup, plus extra for drizzling
1 tsp white wine vinegar
1 tbsp olive oil
1 tsp Magic Roast Chicken Salt (page 244), or just plain sea salt
2 tsp cornflour
150g salted pretzels, crushed to fine crumbs
½ tsp garlic powder
1 tsp smoked paprika

For the broccoli slaw
1 head of broccoli
3 spring onions, finely sliced
20g fresh parsley, finely chopped
120g sultanas or raisins
100g pumpkin seeds
150g vegan mayonnaise
2 tbsp white wine vinegar
2 tbsp Dijon mustard
Fine sea salt and ground black pepper

For serving
2 tbsp American mustard
2 tbsp vegan mayonnaise
4 burger buns, halved
Crinkle cut gherkins (optional)
French fries (optional)

Gotta love a recipe that also doubles as a tongue twister. I just tried to say the name of these sandwiches five times fast and accidentally spat out my false teeth on the first go. Anyway, if you're a lover of sweet/salty combos, the tofu in this recipe will change you fundamentally.

1 Preheat the oven 220°C/Fan 200°C/Gas Mark 7, or air fryer to 200°C.

2 Slice the tofu into triangles about 5mm thick.

3 In a bowl, whisk together the sea salt, Dijon mustard, wholegrain mustard, maple syrup, white wine vinegar, olive oil, Magic Roast Chicken Salt and cornflour. Add the tofu and stir to coat.

4 In a separate bowl, mix the crushed pretzels with the garlic powder and smoked paprika. Dunk the tofu into the pretzel mixture, pressing gently to coat.

5 Place the tofu on a lined baking tray, or in the basket of the air fryer. Bake for 25 minutes, or air-fry for 20 minutes, until crispy and golden.

6 Meanwhile, prepare the broccoli slaw. Chop off the bottom base of the broccoli stalk and peel away the woody outer layers. Break the broccoli into tiny florets, then finely julienne the stalk and any remaining stems.

7 Add to a bowl with the spring onions, parsley, sultanas and pumpkin seeds. Stir in the vegan mayonnaise, white wine vinegar and Dijon mustard and season with sea salt and black pepper.

8 Assemble the sandwiches by spreading the American mustard and mayonnaise on the base of the buns. Place the pretzel-crusted tofu in the burger buns and drizzle with extra maple syrup. Top with the broccoli slaw and gherkins (if using). Serve with fries, if you like.

Serves 4

Prep time:
10 minutes

Cooking time:
25 minutes

Squash 'n' Sausage Tray Bake

1 small butternut squash, peeled and sliced (about 450g prepared weight)
1 large red onion, sliced
10 vegan sausages
300g cherry tomatoes
2 tbsp olive oil
2 tsp dried oregano
1 tsp cumin seeds
1 tsp chilli flakes (optional)
1 tbsp maple syrup
1 tsp flaky sea salt
1 x 250g pouch microwave mixed grains
A handful of fresh coriander, roughly chopped
Juice of ½ lemon

Butternut squash roasts and caramelises so quickly, making it ideal for tray bakes. I've used vegan sausages as the protein here, but if you're not a fan, feel free to replace them with batons of tofu or tempeh. The big flavour of this recipe comes mostly from the herbs and spices, so it'll taste delicious whichever protein you use.

1 Preheat the oven to 220°C/Fan 200°C/Gas Mark 7.

2 Arrange the squash, red onion and vegan sausages on a large baking tray. Scatter over the cherry tomatoes.

3 Drizzle with olive oil, then sprinkle over the oregano, cumin seeds, chilli flakes, if using, maple syrup, and sea salt. Toss everything together to coat evenly.

4 Roast for 20 minutes, shaking the tray halfway through cooking.

5 Add the grains straight from the pouch, stir everything together and return to the oven for 5 minutes.

6 Scatter over the fresh coriander and squeeze over the lemon juice before serving.

(image on previous spread)

Serves 4 | Prep time: 10 minutes | Cooking time: 20 minutes

Tray Bake Tofu Tinga Tacos

450g extra-firm tofu, drained
150ml boiling water
1 vegetable stock cube
1 tbsp olive oil, plus extra for brushing the tacos
2 tsp garlic granules (or 1½ tsp garlic powder)
1 tsp onion granules (or ½ tsp onion powder)
1½ tbsp chipotle paste
1 tsp dried oregano
½ tsp ground cumin
1 tbsp smoked paprika
4 tbsp tomato purée
1 tbsp dark soy sauce
2 tbsp brown sugar
1 tsp fine sea salt
12 small tortillas (corn or wheat)

For serving
4 radishes, finely sliced
Small bunch of fresh coriander, finely chopped
Pickled Pink Onions (page 246) or sliced red onion
Cheat's Salsa Macha (page 247)
1 lime, cut into wedges

Taco Tuesday in record time! These zingy little crispy fellas take 20 minutes in the oven, with no need to pre-cook the deliciously meaty filling. And what's more, everyone can customise their own fillings, so dinner will be more of a family fiesta than family feud!

1 Preheat the oven to 200°C/Fan 180°C/Gas Mark 6.

2 Using the large holes on a box grater, shred the tofu into a medium bowl.

3 In a separate small bowl, pour the boiling water over the stock cube and stir to dissolve. Add the olive oil, garlic and onion granules, chipotle paste, oregano, cumin, smoked paprika, tomato purée, soy sauce, brown sugar and sea salt to the stock.

4 Pour the sauce over the shredded tofu and gently stir until the tofu is evenly coated.

5 Lay the tortillas out on a large baking sheet and divide the tofu filling evenly among them. Gently fold each taco to enclose the filling (you may need to microwave the tortillas for 20 seconds to make them more pliable). Brush the tacos with a little extra olive oil.

6 Place the tacos in the oven and bake for 20 minutes, carefully flipping them halfway through.

7 Serve hot, with radishes, coriander, pickled pink onions, salsa macha, and lime wedges on the side for each person to customise their tacos.

(image overleaf)

DIAL IT UP!

Add some bright acidity with some Pickled Pink Onions (page 246) or dial up the heat with some Cheat's Salsa Macha (page 247)!

Serves 4

Prep time:
10 minutes

Cooking time:
30 minutes

Roasted Carrot Pasta

- 450g carrots (around 4 carrots), peeled and sliced into coins
- 1 medium onion, roughly chopped
- 2 tbsp olive oil
- 1 tbsp miso paste (white or red)
- ½ tsp fine sea salt
- ¼ tsp ground black pepper
- 1 bulb garlic
- 160ml vegetable stock
- 150g silken tofu
- 1 tbsp tomato purée
- 6 sun-dried tomatoes from a jar
- 1 tsp paprika
- 340g dried vegan pasta
- Fresh parsley, finely chopped, to serve
- Chilli flakes, to serve

Carrots and pasta don't hang out together enough, considering how well they get along. In this recipe, we roast up a bunch of carrots that have been massaged with miso paste, then blend to make a sauce that hugs the rigatoni like a long-lost friend. It's sweet and smoky, like an elevated mac and cheese, but without the mac or the cheese.

1 Preheat the oven to 220°C/Fan 200°C/Gas Mark 7.

2 Place the sliced carrots and onion in a large baking tray and drizzle with half of the olive oil. Add the miso paste and massage into the carrots with your hands. Sprinkle with the salt and black pepper.

3 Slice the bulb of garlic in half horizontally and place it in the centre of the carrots, cut-sides up. Drizzle with the remaining olive oil.

4 Place the tray in the oven to roast for 30 minutes, tossing the carrots and onion half-way through cooking, or until the carrots are tender and slightly browned.

5 Remove from the oven and allow to cool for 5 minutes. Squeeze the soft roasted garlic cloves out of their skins into the tray with the carrots.

6 In a blender, combine the roasted carrots, onions and garlic with the vegetable stock, silken tofu, tomato purée, sun-dried tomatoes and paprika, and season with salt and black pepper. Blend until smooth and creamy.

7 Cook the pasta in a large saucepan of salted water until it's al dente. Reserving around a cup of the pasta water, drain and return the pasta to the pan.

8 Pour the creamy sauce over the pasta and place the saucepan back over medium heat. If necessary, use the reserved pasta water to loosen the sauce. Stir until just piping hot, then divide the pasta amongst four bowls. Serve immediately, sprinkled with fresh parsley and chilli flakes.

Serves 4

Prep time:
15 minutes

Cooking time:
40 minutes

Baked Miso Mushroom Rice

150g shiitake mushrooms, roughly chopped
2 tbsp olive oil
½ tsp flaky sea salt
1 onion, peeled and diced
2 large garlic cloves, minced
130g chestnut mushrooms, roughly cubed
200g arborio risotto rice or sushi rice
80ml red wine (ensure it's vegan)
600ml mushroom stock or vegetable stock
2 tbsp miso paste
3 spring onions, finely sliced
1 tsp toasted sesame oil
1 tsp rice vinegar

Risotto is great, but I've always felt it needed some textural variation. I know, sorry Italy, I'm hard to please. This recipe is essentially a baked mushroom risotto, which means it doesn't require any stirring or monitoring, plus it's texturally very varied. The base is silky smooth while the top is crisp and caramelised. We've even got extra roasted shiitake mushrooms in a tangy spring onion dressing. Go on. I dare you to call this one boring.

1 Preheat the oven to 220°C/Fan 200°C/Gas Mark 7.

2 In a medium bowl, toss the shiitake mushrooms with 1 tablespoon of the olive oil and the flaky sea salt. Spread them out on a small baking tray and set aside.

3 Heat the remaining 1 tablespoon olive oil in a large oven-safe frying pan or cast-iron skillet (ensure it fits in your oven) over medium heat.

4 Add the onion and garlic to the pan and fry for 3-4 minutes until starting to brown. Add the chestnut mushrooms and fry until softened and slightly browned, about 3 minutes more. Stir in the rice and toast for 1 minute.

5 Deglaze the pan with the red wine, stirring briefly. Add the stock and miso paste, using a spatula to break up the miso before stirring to combine. Bring the mixture to a rolling simmer, then transfer the pan to the preheated oven.

6 Bake for 10 minutes. Open the oven and place the tray of shiitake mushrooms on a separate shelf. Bake for a further 20 minutes, or until the top of the rice is golden and slightly crispy. Keep an eye on the tray of shiitake mushrooms to prevent burning.

7 Remove the pan and tray from the oven. Top the shiitake mushrooms with the spring onions and drizzle with toasted sesame oil and rice vinegar. Toss with two forks to coat.

8 Top the crispy baked mushroom rice with the dressed shiitake mushrooms and serve hot. Be careful - the frying pan, including the handle, will be very hot.

Serves 4

Prep time:
5 minutes

Cooking time:
25 minutes

All-In Harissa-Roasted Gnocchi

2 x 500g packets gnocchi (ensure it's a vegan variety)
1 red pepper, deseeded and sliced
300g cherry tomatoes
150g green olives
1 x 400g can chickpeas, drained
4 shallots, sliced
3 garlic cloves, finely sliced
2 tbsp olive oil
2 tbsp harissa paste
1 tbsp ras el hanout
3 tbsp nutritional yeast
80g fresh baby spinach

For serving
100g unsweetened, unflavoured vegan yoghurt,
30g roasted unsalted almonds, roughly chopped
10g fresh parsley, destemmed and roughly chopped

Gnocchi is ideal for a quick dinner because it doesn't need to be boiled before being roasted. Just open the pack, dump it in a roasting tin with the rest of the ingredients and whistle a merry tune while the oven does all the hard work. One thing to keep an eye on is your brand of gnocchi! Many use milk and some fresh ones use eggs, so check the ingredients. I use De Cecco brand gnocchi, since they make theirs without either.

1 Preheat the oven to 220°C/Fan 200°C/Gas Mark 7.

2 In a large roasting tray, toss the gnocchi, red pepper, cherry tomatoes, green olives, chickpeas, shallots and garlic with the olive oil, harissa paste, ras el hanout and nutritional yeast. Ensure everything is evenly coated and spread in a single layer.

3 Roast in the oven for 20–25 minutes, stirring halfway through cooking, until the tomatoes are bursting and the gnocchi is lightly browned.

4 Remove the tray from the oven and stir through the fresh baby spinach until just wilted.

5 Serve drizzled with the vegan yoghurt and topped with the roasted almonds and fresh parsley.

(image on previous spread)

Serves 4

Prep time: 5 minutes

Cooking time: 35 minutes

Roasted Shallot and Kimchi Macaroni

250g pearl shallots, quartered
4 garlic cloves, crushed
1½ tbsp olive oil
1 tbsp white miso paste
1½ tbsp white wine vinegar
3 tbsp nutritional yeast
300g vegan kimchi, roughly chopped
380g dried macaroni
850ml boiling hot vegetable stock
150g unsweetened, unflavoured vegan yoghurt
2 tbsp finely chopped fresh chives, to serve

One summer I got obsessed with a pasta sauce I called 'Smashta' (which you might remember, if you follow me on instagram). It just involved roasting fresh tomatoes and garlic in olive oil, then mashing the garlic and whisking in the juices from the tomatoes to create an emulsion. It's still one of my favourites, but out of season tomatoes just don't work for Smashta, so I needed a winter alternative. This one makes use of the sweet subtlety of shallots in place of tomatoes, and guess what? It's also a one-pot dinner, since the pasta is cooked in the roasting tin with the shallots. I haven't come up with an equally catchy name for it yet, but 'Shallotsta' seems to be the natural choice.

1 Preheat the oven to 220°C/Fan 200°C/Gas Mark 7.

2 Place the shallots and garlic in a roasting tin. Add the olive oil, miso paste, white wine vinegar, nutritional yeast and kimchi. Stir until the shallots are evenly coated (it's easiest to do this with your hands). Roast for 20 minutes.

3 Add the dried macaroni and pour in the hot vegetable stock. Stir to combine, then return the tin to the oven and bake for 15 minutes, or until the pasta is tender.

4 Remove from the oven and stir through the vegan yoghurt until creamy.

5 Top with finely chopped chives before serving.

(image overleaf)

Serves 4

Prep time:
5 minutes

Cooking time:
15 minutes

Tempeh Pad Kra Pao

1 tbsp vegetable oil
6 garlic cloves, finely minced
3-4 red bird's eye chillies, finely chopped (adjust to taste), plus extra to serve
3 shallots, finely diced
400g tempeh, crumbled
1 tbsp dark soy sauce
1 tbsp light soy sauce
1 tbsp brown sugar
100ml vegetable stock
40g fresh Thai basil leaves (or holy basil, if available)
Cooked jasmine rice, to serve

Pad kra pao is a super popular Thai stir fry, made traditionally with ground meat and lots of fresh holy basil. It's spicy, aniseed-y and (most importantly) super quick and easy to make. I'm using crumbled tempeh, but you can use crumbled tofu or vegan mince instead, should you desire. The fastest way to crumble tempeh is to roughly grate it with a box grater, but you'll get bigger, less uniform chunks if you pull it apart by hand.

1 Heat the oil in a wok or large frying pan over medium-high heat. Stir in the garlic, chillies and shallots. Cook for 1-2 minutes until fragrant and lightly browned.

2 Add the crumbled tempeh and stir-fry until golden and crispy.

3 Add the dark soy sauce, light soy sauce, brown sugar and vegetable stock. Stir well to coat the tempeh evenly and cook for 1-2 minutes, or until most of the liquid has been absorbed.

4 Toss in the Thai basil leaves and stir until just wilted, about 30 seconds. Remove from the heat immediately.

5 Spoon the pad kra pao over freshly cooked jasmine rice and garnish with additional basil leaves and chilli if desired.

Serves 6

Prep time:
20 minutes

Cooking time:
20 minutes

Cheese and Chive Scones with Mushroom Gravy

300g self-raising flour, plus optional extra for dusting
20g nutritional yeast
½ tsp baking powder
½ tsp fine sea salt
20g fresh chives, finely chopped
80g vegan butter, plus optional extra to serve
180ml unflavoured, unsweetened plant milk, plus 2 tbsp for brushing
2 tsp miso paste
1 tsp white wine vinegar
Pinch of flaky sea salt
Steamed veggies, to serve

For the mushroom gravy
1 tbsp olive oil
1 medium onion, finely chopped
2 garlic cloves, minced
250g fresh mushrooms, sliced
2 tsp dried thyme
100ml dry white wine (ensure it's vegan)
1 tbsp miso paste
2 tbsp nutritional yeast
2 tbsp plain flour
500ml unsweetened soy milk
½ tsp ground black pepper

Don't be daunted by the idea of scones for dinner. I know in the UK savoury scones are rare, but I'm using them here like an American biscuit; essentially just a vessel for gravy, which can only be a good thing. There's no actual cheese (vegan or otherwise) in this recipe, but I promise you, these scones are one of the most deliciously cheesy savoury bakes I've ever pulled off.

1 To make the scones, preheat the oven to 220°C/Fan 200°C/Gas Mark 7 and line a baking sheet with baking paper.

2 Mix the flour, nutritional yeast, baking powder, salt and chives in a medium bowl.

3 Use the large holes of a box grater to shred the vegan butter into the flour mixture. Stir together until the shreds of butter are evenly distributed but still visible.

4 In a measuring jug, mix together the plant milk, miso paste and vinegar. Add to the flour mixture and stir together just until a very rough, shaggy dough comes together.

5 Using a cookie scoop, form eight roughly equal-sized mounds of the dough directly on the lined baking sheet. Alternatively, for more uniform scones, roll out the dough to a rough square on a lightly floured surface and use an 8-9cm round cookie cutter to cut out six scones. Push the trimmings together and cut out the final two scones before placing on the baking sheet. Brush with plant milk and sprinkle with the flaky sea salt.

6 Bake for 25 minutes until puffed up and golden brown, then remove from the oven and allow to cool slightly.

7 While the scones bake, make the mushroom gravy. Heat the olive oil in a medium frying pan over medium heat. Add the onion and garlic, and sauté for 3-4 minutes until softened and fragrant.

(recipe continues overleaf)

8 Add the mushrooms and thyme to the pan and cook for 8–10 minutes until the mushrooms release their moisture and start to brown.

9 Add the white wine and miso paste and stir to combine. Cook for 2–3 minutes, until the liquid reduces slightly. Add the nutritional yeast and plain flour, stirring well to coat the mushrooms. Cook for 1–2 minutes to remove the raw flour taste.

10 Gradually stir in the soy milk, ensuring there are no lumps. Bring to a gentle simmer and allow the gravy to thicken, about 5–7 minutes, while stirring occasionally. Season with black pepper. Remove from the heat.

11 To serve, halve a scone and spread with a little vegan butter, if you like. Ladle over some mushroom gravy and serve hot. Optionally serve with steamed veggies.

DIAL IT UP!

Swap out the miso paste in the mushroom gravy for Ultimate Umami Paste (page 243).

P

No-Cook Nights

There are nights when cooking feels like a joy - when the whole family chips in, joyfully peeling vegetables and laughing together like a Getty Images stock photo. And then there are real-life non-imaginary nights when even the thought of frying an onion feels like an unreasonable demand. This chapter is for those nights. The nights when you're too tired, too busy, or too hot to generate any extra heat in your kitchen.

These are meals that require zero actual cooking - no frying, no roasting, no standing over a saucepan questioning your life choices. At most, you might need to boil a kettle or zap something in the microwave, but that's as far as the effort goes. Think buttery Gochujang Crabless Rolls (page 205) that basically make themselves. Or maybe my light and refreshing Spicy Beet and Mango Rice Paper Tostadas (page 198) that come together in minutes.

So, whether you're running on fumes after a long day, or you simply refuse to create any more washing up than absolutely necessary, this chapter has your back. Minimum effort, maximum reward!

Serves 2

Prep time:
15 minutes

Shredded Beet Hummus Bowl

120g couscous
1 tsp bouillon powder
180ml boiling water
80g hummus
½ cucumber, sliced
100g Kalamata olives
50g drained canned chickpeas
50g cherry tomatoes, halved
½ red onion, thinly sliced
100g cooked, vacuum-packed beetroot
Warmed flatbreads, to serve

For the dressing
4 tbsp vegan yoghurt
1 small garlic clove, finely minced
1 tbsp white wine vinegar, or lemon juice
1 tbsp olive oil
1 tsp agave syrup
Pinch of fine sea salt
Small bunch fresh parsley, roughly chopped, plus extra to serve

A quick dinner with no cooking required that feels kind of like a salad but also so much more than just a salad. This is the kind of meal I eat when I've just been to the supermarket and have a full fridge but a low battery. It takes virtually no effort and yet feels super nourishing. Right, I'm finally ready to put away the frozen stuff!

1 Place the couscous in a small bowl and stir in the bouillon powder. Pour the boiling water over, cover with a plate and set aside for 5 minutes.

2 While the couscous absorbs the water, arrange the hummus, cucumber, olives, chickpeas, cherry tomatoes and red onion in two serving bowls, leaving a space for the couscous.

3 Use the large holes of a box grater to grate the beetroot directly over the hummus.

4 Place the yoghurt, garlic, white wine vinegar, olive oil, agave syrup, salt and chopped dill in a jar. Secure the lid and shake well.

5 Fluff up the couscous with a fork, then divide it between the two bowls.

6 Drizzle the dressing over everything and scatter over some extra parsley, if desired.

7 Serve with warmed flatbreads on the side.

Serves 2

Prep time:
15 minutes

Speedy Satay Silken Tofu with Smacked Cucumber Salad

For the cucumber salad
1 medium cucumber
Pinch of fine sea salt
1 tbsp soy sauce
1 tbsp rice vinegar
1 tsp toasted sesame oil
1 tbsp Crispy Garlic Chilli Oil (page 245)

For the tofu
300g firm silken tofu
2 tbsp chunky peanut butter (I love Manilife deep roast)
1 tbsp gochujang paste
1 tbsp soy sauce
2 tbsp lime juice
1 tsp maple syrup, or agave syrup
1 tbsp Crispy Garlic Chilli Oil (page 245), plus extra to serve
20g dry roasted peanuts, roughly chopped
1 spring onion, finely sliced

For Serving
1 x 200g microwave pouch of sushi rice, or jasmine rice

Don't fall into the trap of hating silken tofu because it's soft instead of crispy. This recipe celebrates the velvety smooth texture of silken tofu by bathing it in a thick, spicy, peanutty sauce. You're also going to love how fast this recipe is to get on the table. It's a true mid-week miracle.

1 Smack the cucumber with the flat side of a knife or rolling pin until it splits, then tear into chunks. Toss with the sea salt and set aside for 5 minutes.

2 Meanwhile, in a medium bowl, whisk together the soy sauce, rice vinegar, toasted sesame oil and crispy garlic chilli oil.

3 Drain off any liquid the cucumber has released. Add the cucumber to the dressing, toss to coat, then set aside.

4 For the tofu, gently cut the silken tofu into thick slices and arrange on a serving plate. Heat the rice in the microwave according to the package instructions or, if you'd prefer, serve cold. Divide the rice between the two plates.

5 In a bowl, whisk together the peanut butter, gochujang, soy sauce, lime juice, maple syrup and crispy garlic chilli oil until smooth.

6 Spoon the satay sauce over the tofu. Top with extra crispy garlic chilli oil, the chopped peanuts and sliced spring onion.

7 Serve alongside the smacked cucumber salad.

Serves 2

Prep time:
15 minutes

Pink Poke Bowl

340g jar pickled beetroot
1 x 250g pouch microwave sticky rice
2 tsp rice vinegar
½ tsp sugar
¼ tsp sea salt
70g baby sweetcorn
100g cooked, shelled edamame
4 radishes, finely sliced
40g macadamia nuts
2 spring onions, finely sliced

For the sauce
3 tbsp vegan mayonnaise
1 tsp lime juice
1 tsp sriracha
1 tsp beetroot vinegar

For serving
Fresh coriander
Pickled sushi ginger
Sesame seeds

This recipe came about by accident when I ran out of sushi vinegar for seasoning cooked rice. Instead, I used the pickling liquid from a jar of beetroot and watched as the rice turned Barbie pink. I almost even called this one 'Barbie Poke' until I realised that 'Pink Poke Bowl' sounds like a fitting tribute to Chappell Roan, so we're running with it.

1 Remove the beetroot from the jar, reserving the pickling liquid, and dice into rough cubes.

2 Microwave the sticky rice according to the package instructions, then spread it out on a plate.

3 In a small bowl, mix together the rice vinegar, sugar, salt and 1 tablespoon of the reserved beetroot pickling liquid. Spoon over the rice and stir to coat until all the rice is pink. Leave to cool fully.

4 Slice the baby sweetcorn into thin coins and place them in the jar with the remaining beetroot pickling liquid. Put the lid on, shake gently, then set aside for at least 10 minutes while you prepare the rest of the poke bowl ingredients.

5 In a small bowl, stir together the sauce ingredients and set aside.

6 To serve, divide the pink rice between two bowls and top with the cubed beetroot, pink pickled baby sweetcorn, edamame, radishes, macadamia nuts, and spring onions. Drizzle with the sauce and garnish with fresh coriander, pickled sushi ginger and sesame seeds before serving.

Serves 2

Prep time:
10 minutes

Spicy Beet and Mango Rice Paper Tostadas

4 rice paper sheets
1 tbsp vegetable oil
1 tbsp mild chilli powder
250g cooked beetroot, drained
160g fresh mango
1 tsp soy sauce
1 tsp rice vinegar, or white wine vinegar
1 tsp mirin
1 tbsp sriracha
1 tsp sesame oil
4 tbsp vegan mayonnaise
¼ sheet nori seaweed, cut into fine threads
Toasted black sesame seeds, to serve

Rice paper discs, usually used for spring rolls, turn to puffed, crispy crackers with just a minute in the microwave. It's like stepping into a phone booth in a tracksuit and leaving in a wedding dress. The topping is inspired by spicy tuna sushi rolls with a kick of sweet, tangy mango.

1 Brush the rice paper sheets with vegetable oil. One sheet at a time, place in the microwave and cook for 1 minute, watching closely to make sure they don't brown or burn. Repeat until all the rice paper sheets are puffed and crispy. Sprinkle with chilli powder and break each sheet into quarters, then set aside.

2 Slice the beetroot and mango into 5mm cubes and transfer to a bowl. Add the soy sauce, rice vinegar, mirin, sriracha, sesame oil and vegan mayonnaise, then mix together.

3 Right before serving, top the rice paper sheets with the spicy beet and mango mixture, then top with the nori seaweed and toasted black sesame seeds.

Serves 2

Prep time:
10 minutes

Spicy Tahini Lime Noodles

190g thin rice noodles
40g kale, destemmed and roughly chopped
1 tsp toasted sesame oil
2 tbsp tahini paste
2 tsp gochujang (or substitute with harissa paste)
2 tbsp soy sauce (or substitute with tamari sauce)
2 tbsp lime juice
1 small garlic clove, finely minced
½ tbsp minced fresh ginger
160g cooked edamame beans
½ cucumber, sliced
2 spring onions, sliced
2 tsp crispy chilli oil (shop-bought or see page 245, optional)
1 tsp sesame seeds

It's been one of those days where you blinked somewhere around 9.45am and somehow it's now 8.30pm. It's an orange alert for hanger outbursts and that out-of-date granola bar in your handbag barely touched the sides. Luckily this nutritious dinner requires zero cooking and can be on the table in ten minutes. Crisis averted!

1. Place the rice noodles in a large bowl and cover with boiling water. Let them soak for 5–7 minutes, or until tender. Drain and set aside.
2. While the noodles are soaking, put the kale in a separate bowl, drizzle with toasted sesame oil and massage until it softens slightly.
3. In a small bowl, mix together the tahini, gochujang, soy sauce, lime juice, garlic and ginger to create a creamy dressing.
4. Add the drained noodles to the bowl with the kale. Pour the dressing over the noodles and toss everything together until well coated.
5. Divide the dressed noodles between two bowls. Top each bowl with half of the edamame, cucumber slices, spring onion, crispy chilli oil, if using, and sesame seeds.
6. Serve warm or cold.

Serves 4

Prep time:
12 minutes

Warm Grain and Olive Salad

For the salad
150g marinated green olives, roughly chopped
220g cherry tomatoes, halved
½ red onion, finely sliced
20g fresh coriander, roughly chopped
10g fresh chives, finely sliced
5g fresh dill, roughly chopped
60g roasted unsalted almonds, roughly chopped
100g pomegranate seeds
100g vegan feta, crumbled
1 x 250g pouch microwave mixed grains
Flatbreads or toasted ciabatta, to serve (optional)

For the dressing
2 tbsp caramelised red onion chutney
2 tbsp extra-virgin olive oil
2 tbsp red wine vinegar
Zest and juice of ½ lemon
2 tsp harissa paste
1 tsp Dijon mustard
½ tsp ground black pepper
½ tsp fine sea salt

If I'm having salad for a main meal, it's got to be a big one. I don't just mean big in scale, but in flavour and texture. I'm talking big juicy olives with warm toasty grains, bright cherry tomatoes and crunchy roasted almonds. But the real star of this salad is the dressing. I used to make it by frying onions until caramelised and sweet, but a few spoons of onion chutney will save you about 15 minutes and the flavour is just as good.

1. In a salad bowl, combine all the salad ingredients except for the grains.
2. Heat the grains in the microwave according to the package instructions, then add to the salad bowl.
3. In a small bowl, whisk together all the dressing ingredients. Pour over the salad and toss to dress.
4. Serve warm, optionally with flatbreads or slices of toasted ciabatta, if you like.

(image on previous spread)

Makes
4 rolls

Prep time:
10 minutes

Gochujang Crabless Rolls

1 small garlic clove, finely minced
Zest and juice of ½ lemon
½ tsp fine sea salt
1½ tbsp gochujang paste
1 tsp Dijon mustard
140g vegan mayonnaise
10g fresh chives, finely chopped, plus extra for serving
1 shallot, finely sliced
½ tsp ground black pepper
¼ tsp celery salt, or fine sea salt
450g extra-firm tofu, drained
4 hot dog buns
1 head baby gem lettuce

This protein-packed sandwich filling is ready in literally minutes and all you need is a cheese grater. Be sure to use extra-firm tofu and, if you can, let the filling chill in the fridge for a bit before assembly, to allow the flavours to develop. If you don't have hot dog buns (and you don't fear the ire of people from New England) this filling works well in wraps, on flatbreads, or just between two doorstop slices of white bread.

1 Place the garlic, lemon zest, lemon juice and salt in a medium bowl and stir together. Set aside for a minute (the lemon juice takes the raw edge off the garlic).

2 Add the gochujang, mustard, vegan mayonnaise, chives, shallot, pepper and celery salt to the bowl and whisk until smooth.

3 Use the large holes on a box grater to shred the tofu into the bowl, then stir to combine.

4 Slice the hot dog buns down the middle and fill with a few leaves of lettuce.

5 Divide the filling between the buns and top with a little black pepper and the extra chives before serving.

(image overleaf)

Serves 2

Prep time:
15 minutes

Chicory, Shaved Fennel and Grapefruit Panzanella

2 thick slices sourdough bread
2 chicory heads (red, white or one of each)
1 medium fennel bulb
150g vegan feta
1 grapefruit
1 garlic clove, minced
4 tbsp extra-virgin olive oil
1 tbsp white wine vinegar
2 tsp Dijon mustard
2 tsp maple syrup
1 tsp flaky sea salt
½ tsp ground black pepper
A handful of fresh basil leaves
Small bunch of fresh dill, torn

Traditional panzanella, made with fresh, juicy tomatoes, is a staple for me throughout summer. But what happens in autumn? Panzanella cold turkey? Not if I can help it! The seasonal stars align in mid-autumn with chicory, fennel and grapefruit all at their best, so why not make the most of those big, bitter-sweet flavours instead? As with all panzanellas, stale bread works best, but keep an eye on it in the toaster, or you'll find yourself wafting a tea towel at the smoke alarm.

1. Toast the sourdough bread in a toaster until golden and crisp. Allow to cool, then tear into bite-sized cubes. Place in a large salad bowl.
2. Roughly tear the chicory into individual leaves and add to the salad bowl.
3. Trim the fennel bulb, reserving any fronds for garnish, and use a mandoline or sharp knife to shave it thinly. Crumble the vegan feta and add to the salad bowl with the fennel.
4. Peel and segment the grapefruit. Cut the segments from the membrane and add all but two of the segments to the salad. Squeeze the juice from the reserved segments into a separate small bowl.
5. To the same small bowl, add the garlic, extra-virgin olive oil, white wine vinegar, Dijon mustard, maple syrup, flaky sea salt and ground black pepper.
6. Drizzle the dressing over the salad and toss gently to combine.
7. Scatter the fresh basil and dill over the salad. Serve immediately.

Serves 4

Prep time:
10 minutes

Sriracha 'Tuna' Pasta Salad

370g cooked vegan pasta (around 200g uncooked)
140g grilled artichoke hearts, roughly chopped
1 red onion, finely diced
1 red pepper, deseeded and cubed
120g drained canned sweetcorn
150g cherry tomatoes, halved
Small bunch of fresh dill, roughly chopped
2 tbsp sriracha sauce
2 tsp English mustard
2 tsp white wine vinegar
Juice of ½ lemon
150g vegan yoghurt
65g vegan mayonnaise
¼ tsp fine sea salt
¼ tsp ground black pepper
2 tsp capers, roughly chopped

An easy summer salad with undeniable seafood vibes. Instead of tuna, we're using those pots of grilled artichoke hearts you find in the antipasti section of the supermarket. They're flaky and perfect for soaking up this deliciously creamy, spicy dressing. Any hot sauce will do for this recipe, but sriracha has a uniquely sweet, garlicky flavour that packs a punch.

1 In a large mixing bowl, combine the cooked pasta, grilled artichoke hearts, red onion, red pepper, sweetcorn, cherry tomatoes and dill.

2 In a separate small bowl, whisk together the sriracha, English mustard, white wine vinegar, lemon juice, vegan yoghurt, vegan mayonnaise, sea salt, black pepper and capers until smooth.

3 Pour the dressing over the pasta mixture and toss well to coat all the ingredients evenly.

4 Serve immediately or refrigerate for at least 30 minutes to allow the flavours to develop.

Fast 'n' Sweet

Surprise! Everyone in your house is experiencing synchronised spontaneous dessert cravings (despite the delicious meal you just made) and they're all looking at you like the cat from the meme with the tears in its eyes. So, what's your next move? I don't think fruit salad's going to cut it again, hun.

This chapter is here to help solve your sticky dessert crisis with some fast puds that deliver big on satisfaction. I'm talking about a hot, Ultra-Fudgy Instant Miso Brownie (page 229) which, with the help of the microwave, goes from craving to reality in three minutes flat. Or how about a genius little blueberry pie hack that turns frozen parathas into the flakiest, most perfect pasty (page 230).

Finally! Desserts for the impatient, the unprepared and the insatiable!

Serves 4

Prep time:
10 minutes, plus freezing

Spicy Mango Tamarind Sorbet

- 5 tbsp strawberry jam
- 1½ tbsp tamarind paste
- 1 tbsp lime juice
- 1 tsp Tajin (or ½ tsp mild chilli powder), plus extra to serve
- Pinch of fine sea salt
- 500g frozen mango
- 2 ripe bananas, peeled, sliced and frozen
- 4 tbsp unflavoured, unsweetened plant milk

This recipe is inspired by the Mexican frozen drink Mangonada. It's made from blended mango, layered with a deliciously tangy, spicy fermented fruit paste called '*chamoy*'. In this sorbet recipe, I've tried to replicate the deliciously confusing salty, funky flavour of *chamoy* using tamarind paste, strawberry jam and lime juice. If you can access the famous Tajin seasoning, you're onto a winner, but don't worry if not - use mild chilli powder instead.

1. Place an empty ice cream tub or airtight container in the freezer to chill.
2. In a small bowl, mix together the jam, tamarind paste, lime juice, Tajin and the sea salt.
3. In a food processor, pulse together the mango, bananas and plant milk until creamy, smooth and thick. You may have to stop the food processor and scrape down the sides a few times. Spoon a quarter of the blended mixture into the chilled container, then drizzle with the tamarind mixture. Repeat, layering mango sorbet with tamarind mixture until it is all used up.
4. Place in the freezer for 2 hours, then scoop and serve, sprinkled with a little extra Tajin.

(image on previous spread)

Serves 2

Prep time:
5 minutes

Cooking time:
2 minutes 40 seconds

Microwave Ginger and Maple Syrup Pudding

2 tbsp maple syrup, plus extra for drizzling
2 tbsp vegetable oil
2 tbsp caster sugar
75ml soy milk
1 tbsp ginger paste
¼ tsp vanilla extract
80g self-raising flour
¼ tsp baking soda
Vegan custard or vanilla ice cream, to serve

Syrup pudding was a huge part of my childhood dessert experience, which is weird, because they're such a faff to make and my mum didn't exactly have time to watch a sponge steam for two hours. This one, on the other hand, is very fast and easy, which makes it feel like I'm mainlining nostalgia. I've added some ginger and swapped the golden syrup for maple, to make it even more warm and cuddly.

1 Grease a small, microwave-safe pudding bowl and pour 1 tablespoon of the maple syrup into the bottom.

2 In a separate bowl, mix together the rest of the maple syrup with all the remaining ingredients until just smooth. Pour the pudding batter into the greased bowl.

3 Microwave the pudding on full power for 2 minutes 40 seconds.

4 Remove from the microwave, then immediately invert onto a serving plate and remove the bowl.

5 Drizzle with more maple syrup and serve with vegan custard or vanilla ice cream.

(image overleaf)

Serves 4

Prep time:
10 minutes

Cooking time:
30 minutes

Cheat's Tarte Tatin with Maple and Star Anise

50g vegan butter
100ml maple syrup
3 green apples, peeled, cored and sliced into 1cm wedges
3 star anise
1 x 320g sheet of ready-rolled puff pastry (ensure it's vegan)
Vegan ice cream, to serve

OK, it's a bit rich to call this 'fast and sweet' when it takes 28 minutes to bake, but I promise you, it's still a hell of a lot easier to make than a regular tarte tatin! It's all baked in a skillet or frying pan, so be sure to use one that's oven safe.

1 Preheat the oven to 220°C/Fan 200°C/Gas Mark 7.

2 Place the vegan butter, maple syrup, apple wedges and star anise in a 24cm oven-safe skillet or frying pan. Roast in the oven for 8 minutes.

3 Meanwhile, unroll the puff pastry and cut out a 24cm circle using a plate as a guide.

4 Remove the skillet from the oven and drape the pastry over the apples. Poke a small steam hole in the centre with a knife.

5 Return to the oven and bake for 20 minutes until the pastry is golden and crisp.

6 Let it stand for 2 minutes, then cover the skillet with a plate and carefully invert to reveal the caramelised apples.

7 Remove the star anise and serve warm with a scoop of vegan ice cream.

Makes 8

Prep time:
10 minutes

Cooking time:
15 minutes

Puff Pastry Cinnamon Yum Yums

1 x 320g sheet of ready-rolled puff pastry (ensure it's vegan)
3 tbsp plant milk, plus 1 tsp extra for glaze
2 tbsp caster sugar
1 tsp ground cinnamon
3 tbsp icing sugar

This recipe, like most good ones, started out as a byproduct. Every time I'd bake with puff pastry, I'd use any trimmings to make these for a little dessert. Over time, priorities shifted and yum yums became the reason for buying puff pastry. Pre-rolled pastry is convenient, but never thick enough, in my opinion, so this recipe doubles it up for thick, generous, flaky layers. Enjoy them alone, or dunk in a mug of hot chocolate; either way, they live up to their name.

1 Preheat the oven to 220°C/Fan 200°C/Gas Mark 7. Line a baking sheet with baking paper.

2 Slice the puff pastry sheet in half widthways to create two even rectangles. Brush one rectangle with plant milk, then place the second one on top.

3 In a small bowl, mix together the caster sugar and ground cinnamon.

4 Brush the top of the pastry stack with plant milk and sprinkle with half of the cinnamon sugar. Flip the pastry stack, brush with plant milk, and sprinkle with the remaining cinnamon sugar.

5 Slice the pastry widthways into eight equal strips, then twist each strip into a spiral and place on the prepared baking sheet.

6 Bake for 15 minutes, or until golden brown and puffed up. Remove from the oven and allow to cool to room temperature.

7 In a small bowl, whisk together the icing sugar and 1 teaspoon plant milk until smooth. Drizzle the glaze over the yum yums and serve.

Serves 2

Prep time:
10 mins

Tiramisu Ice Cream Sundae

- 2 tbsp instant coffee granules
- 1 tbsp cocoa powder, plus extra for dusting
- 3 tbsp caster sugar
- 2 tbsp boiling water
- 1 tbsp coffee liqueur
- 50ml espresso (or very strong coffee)
- 8 Lotus Biscoff cookies
- 4 large scoops vegan vanilla ice cream

I'm a massive believer that if you have access to good coffee and a scoop of ice cream, you've got dessert sorted. This recipe takes that idea and runs with it. You'll need to use an electric whisk or a stand mixer to get the creamy dalgona-style coffee whip going, but trust me, it's worth it!

1. In a medium bowl, whip the instant coffee, cocoa powder, caster sugar and boiling water using an electric whisk or stand mixer until creamy, glossy and holding stiff peaks. Set aside.
2. In a small bowl, mix the coffee liqueur and espresso.
3. To assemble, dunk four of the Biscoff cookies into the espresso mixture and place two in the bottom of each of two small bowls or sundae glasses.
4. Top with a scoop of vegan vanilla ice cream and a spoonful of the whipped coffee mixture. Repeat the layers, finishing with a final spoonful of whipped coffee on top.
5. Serve immediately or freeze for up to 30 minutes. Dust with cocoa powder just before serving.

Makes 20

Prep time:
5 minutes, plus cooling

Cooking time:
1 minute

Nutty Golden Nuggets

170g smooth peanut butter
100g golden syrup
115g vegan butter
1 tsp vanilla extract
80g cornflakes
30g toasted coconut flakes
170g roasted unsalted nuts
70g dark chocolate chips (at least 54% cocoa, make sure they're vegan)
Large pinch of flaky sea salt
Gold lustre spray (optional)

I made a batch of these for my family this Christmas and they were so delicious. I haven't stopped making them and it's now March - help! They're similar to *bocaditos* (a Latin American cornflake cake, of sorts), but with nut butter instead of condensed milk. They take a while to cool and set fully, but they keep well in the fridge for up to a week, so they're ideal for a little evening sweet treat.

1 Put the peanut butter, golden syrup, vegan butter and vanilla extract in a microwave-proof measuring jug or bowl and place in the microwave. Heat in 15-second bursts, stirring well after each go, until smooth and glossy (this took me a total of 1 minute).

2 Mix together the cornflakes, toasted coconut flakes, roasted nuts, chocolate chips and flaky sea salt in a medium bowl. Add the peanut butter mixture and stir to combine, being careful not to break up too many cornflakes.

3 Spoon heaped dessertspoons of the mixture onto a baking sheet lined with baking paper. If you'd like more regular shaped nuggets, spoon into a small cookie cutter placed on the baking paper, push gently into shape, then remove and repeat. Alternatively, spoon into cupcake cases. Spray the top of the nuggets with the gold lustre spray, if using.

4 Place the nuggets in the fridge to cool and set for at least an hour. If not serving immediately, transfer the cooled nuggets to an airtight container and keep in the fridge for up to a week.

Serves 2

Prep time:
2 minutes

Cooking time:
1 minute 45 seconds

Ultra-Fudgy Instant Miso Brownie

3 tbsp cocoa powder
3 tbsp plain flour
¼ tsp baking powder
3 tbsp caster sugar
Pinch of fine sea salt
4 tbsp unflavoured, unsweetened plant milk
2 tbsp vegetable oil
¼ tsp vanilla extract
1 tsp white miso paste
2 tbsp dark chocolate chips (at least 54% cocoa, make sure they're vegan), plus 1 tbsp extra for topping (or use a roughly chopped bar of dark chocolate)
Vegan vanilla ice cream, to serve

A fresh, warm brownie in under four minutes sounds like witchcraft, but it's not. It's microwave magic. I'll admit, I've always been sceptical of microwaved desserts (probably PTSD from my first ever job microwaving Costco fudge cakes in my local pub for £3 per hour), but this was unfounded. This brownie is fudgy yet somehow incredibly light, with a flutter of umami from the miso paste. It works in a small dish as a two-person dessert, or divide the batter into two mugs if you're not great at sharing.

1. Mix together all the ingredients in a medium bowl to make the batter.
2. Transfer to a small microwaveable dish, spread into an even layer and top with the extra chocolate chips.
3. Microwave on full power for 1 minute 45 seconds.
4. Remove from the microwave and top with a generous scoop of vegan ice cream before serving with two spoons.

Serves 2

Prep time:
10 minutes

Cooking time:
30 minutes

Blueberry Paratha Pies

2 frozen parathas
140g frozen blueberries
80g apricot jam
1 tsp cornflour
2 tbsp plant milk
½ tbsp granulated sugar
¼ tsp ground cinnamon
Vegan vanilla ice cream, to serve

My freezer is never without three things: frozen blueberries (for smoothies), vegan ice cream (for emergencies) and frozen parathas (for everything else). Combine all three like a Power Rangers megazord and you get these crispy, flaky blueberry pies that can be made ahead and baked from frozen. And since we're using pre-rolled, circular parathas, there's no trimming and no wasted pastry. They almost have the texture of McDonalds apple pies but with a way less offensively sweet filling.

1 Preheat the oven to 220°C/200°C Fan/Gas Mark 7 and line a baking sheet with baking paper.

2 Remove the parathas from the freezer and take off the top layer of plastic from each. Let them defrost for 5 minutes.

3 In a medium bowl, mix the frozen blueberries, apricot jam and cornflour until combined.

4 Divide the blueberry filling evenly between the two parathas. Keeping the bottom layer of plastic attached, fold each paratha over to enclose the filling, and pinch the edges to seal.

5 Carefully peel away the bottom layer of plastic. (If the paratha tears, place it in the freezer for 5 minutes before trying again.) Place the pies on the prepared baking sheet and brush with plant milk.

6 In a small bowl, combine the sugar and cinnamon, then sprinkle over the pies.

7 Bake for 30 minutes, or until the pies are golden brown and crispy. Allow to cool for 5 minutes before serving with vegan ice cream.

8 Alternatively, place the unbaked pies in the freezer until firm, then transfer to an airtight container and keep frozen for up to 3 months. When you're ready, bake from frozen for 35 minutes at 220°C/200°C Fan/Gas Mark 7.

Serves 2

Prep time:
10 minutes

Cooking time:
20 minutes

Roasted Pineapple and Coconut Trifles

500g frozen pineapple chunks (or use fresh or canned pineapple)
4 tbsp light brown sugar
½ tsp ground cinnamon
½ tsp ground ginger
2 tbsp coconut rum
2 tbsp lime juice
12 ginger nut cookies

For the coconut cream
1 x 160ml can coconut cream, chilled (or 110ml vegan double cream)
50g vegan coconut yoghurt
1 tbsp agave syrup or maple syrup
½ tbsp lime juice

For decorating
1 ginger nut cookie
4 tbsp toasted flaked coconut
Zest of 1 lime, finely grated

Something special happens when you roast pineapple. It goes from bright and tropical to warm and comforting. Combine it with nutty ginger cookies and whipped coconut cream and you've got a rather majestic dessert.

1 Preheat your oven to 200°C/180°C Fan/Gas Mark 6. Toss the pineapple chunks with the light brown sugar, ground cinnamon and ground ginger in a medium mixing bowl. Spread the pineapple in a single layer on a baking tray lined with baking paper and roast in the oven for 20 minutes, stirring halfway through cooking, until golden and caramelized. Remove from the oven and set aside to cool.

2 While the pineapple is roasting, prepare the coconut cream. Scoop the thick cream from the top of the chilled can and place in the bowl of a stand mixer or a large mixing bowl if using an electric whisk. Whip the cream on high speed until stiff peaks and then add the other ingredients. Whisk again until smooth and fully combined. Set aside.

3 In a medium bowl, combine the coconut rum and lime juice to create a soaking liquid for the ginger nut cookies. Dunk six cookies into the rum mixture, one at a time, allowing each to soak briefly without falling apart.

4 Begin assembling the trifles in two small serving bowls or glasses. Add a quarter of the roasted pineapple to the bottom of each bowl. Place three soaked ginger nut cookies on top of the pineapple layer in each bowl. Spoon a quarter of the whipped coconut cream mixture over the cookies to create the first layer.

5 Repeat the process with another layer of pineapple, three more soaked ginger nut cookies, and the remaining whipped coconut cream mixture.

6 If you're not serving immediately, cover the bowls with cling film and refrigerate for a few hours or overnight.

7 Grate the reserved ginger nut cookie over the top of each trifle to serve. Sprinkle with toasted coconut flakes and finish with a dusting of finely grated lime zest.

Serves 2

Prep time:
5 minutes

Cooking time:
10 minutes

Rum and Raisin Bananas Foster

30g pecans, roughly chopped
60g vegan butter
150g dark brown sugar
½ tsp ground cinnamon
2 ripe bananas, peeled and halved lengthwise
50g flame raisins
50ml spiced rum
Vegan vanilla ice cream, to serve

This is one of those desserts that's so delicious it just makes you chuckle (or maybe that's just the rum?). It's an American classic of caramelised bananas with (a lot of) brown sugar and cinnamon, combined with my undying love for anything 'rum 'n' raisin'. Ice cream is a must, for serving, and I also urge you not to use rubbish raisins. Treat yourself to a pack of big fat flame raisins. You won't regret it.

1 Place a large frying pan over medium heat and toast the pecans until lightly golden and fragrant. Remove from the pan and set aside.

2 Add the vegan butter, sugar and cinnamon to the pan at the same time, stirring until the sugar dissolves and the mixture is bubbling.

3 Place the bananas in the pan, cut sides down, and cook for 2 minutes until softened and lightly caramelised. Gently turn the bananas over and cook for another minute.

4 Add the raisins and spiced rum to the pan, stirring gently to combine. Allow the sauce to simmer for a minute until thickened.

5 Remove the pan from the heat and sprinkle the toasted pecans over the top.

6 Serve immediately with scoops of vegan vanilla ice cream, drizzling the sauce over the bananas and ice cream.

Serves 4 | Prep time: 5 minutes | Cooking time: 20 minutes

Gnocchi Pretending to be Churros

2 tbsp vegan butter, melted (or vegetable oil)
500g fresh gnocchi (make sure it's a vegan variety, like De Cecco)
4 tbsp caster sugar
2 tsp ground cinnamon
160ml coconut cream
160g dark chocolate (at least 54% cocoa, make sure it's vegan), finely chopped

In my house, this recipe goes by its alternative title, 'Dessert Pasta'. Sounds a little jarring, but trust me, they're irresistible. When coated in cinnamon sugar, light and fluffy gnocchi dumplings become cousins to churros. Skewer and dunk in dark chocolate ganache to complete the experience.

1 Heat a medium frying pan over medium heat and add the vegan butter. Once melted, add the gnocchi and fry for 10 minutes, tossing regularly, until golden brown.

2 While the gnocchi cook, mix together the sugar and cinnamon in a medium bowl.

3 In a separate microwave-safe bowl or measuring jug, combine the coconut cream and finely chopped chocolate. Heat in the microwave in 30-second bursts, stirring well after each one, until you have a smooth, glossy chocolate ganache.

4 Transfer the gnocchi to a baking sheet or large plate. Immediately sprinkle with the cinnamon sugar and turn to make sure they're coated on all sides.

5 Serve hot with the bowl of chocolate ganache. Use bamboo skewers or a fork to make dunking easier.

Dinner Dial-Ups

I've been accused, once or twice, of having a condiment addiction. My favourite vacation activity is going to a foreign supermarket and filling my suitcase with, you guessed it, condiments. And sure, there have been moments when I've opened the fridge to find it full of sauces, spreads and syrups, but nothing to put them on, but hey, we all have our vices! I think a meal can be made or broken by the condiments you choose to serve it with.

My Dinner Dial-Ups are a selection of quick, simple recipes for making your own flavour-bomb condiments that will transform practically any dinner into something dramatically more majestic. Like that scene in *Beauty and the Beast* where the beast turns back into a human. Except famously the beast gets less cute as a human. OK bad metaphor, but you get the idea.

All of these recipes make enough for multiple servings, and they can sit in the fridge until you're ready to use them. Throughout the book, I'll put a 'Dial It Up!' box at the bottom of any recipes that I think can be taken to the next level with one of my homemade condiments. Like my Courgette and Green Bean Stir Fry (see page 34), which absolutely *sings* with a spoonful of my Ultimate Umami Paste (see page 243) stirred through. You'll also occasionally find a Dinner Dial-Up listed as a required ingredient, but don't worry, I'll also provide a store-bought substitution, just in case you don't have time to make your own.

Makes 4–6 servings | Prep time: 5 minutes | Cooking time: 10 minutes

Crispy Rosemary Pangrattato

100g stale bread (or 50g panko breadcrumbs)
1 tbsp olive oil
½ tbsp finely chopped fresh rosemary
1 garlic clove, minced
¼ tsp flaky sea salt
Zest of 1 lemon, finely grated

1 Tear or cut the bread into small chunks and pulse in a food processor until it forms coarse crumbs. Alternatively, grate the bread by hand for a rustic texture. (If using breadcrumbs, skip this step.)

2 Heat the olive oil in a frying pan over medium heat. Add the breadcrumbs and toast, stirring constantly, for 2–3 minutes until they start to crisp.

3 Stir in the rosemary and garlic, cooking for another 1–2 minutes until fragrant and golden brown.

4 Season with the salt and stir in the lemon zest.

5 Remove from the heat and let cool. Use immediately or store in an airtight container for up to 3 days.

Makes
2-4 servings

Prep time:
5 minutes

Tofu Crème Fraîche

300g soft silken tofu
1 tbsp miso paste
Pinch of fine sea salt
Pinch of caster sugar
1 tbsp white wine vinegar

1 Blend all the ingredients together - a regular blender or immersion blender both work well.

2 Use immediately or transfer to a clean jar and cover with a lid. Store in the fridge for up to a week.

Makes
about 390g

Prep time:
5 minutes

High-Protein Ranch Dressing

300g silken tofu, drained
1 tbsp extra-virgin olive oil
1½ tbsp white wine vinegar
50g vegan mayonnaise
½ teaspoon garlic granules
½ teaspoon onion granules
½ teaspoon celery salt
¼ teaspoon ground white pepper
1 teaspoon dried chives
1 teaspoon dried parsley
½ teaspoon dried dill
½ tsp sugar
½ tsp fine sea salt

1 Place all the ingredients in a blender and blend until smooth.

2 Transfer to an airtight container and place in the fridge for at least 30 minutes to allow the flavours to develop.

3 If not using immediately, store in the fridge for up to a week.

(image opposite)

Makes
about 260ml

Prep time:
5 minutes

Quick Ketchup

200g tomato purée
2 tbsp agave syrup, or maple syrup
3 tbsp white wine vinegar
1 tsp onion powder
½ tsp celery salt
½ tsp garlic powder
½ tsp finely ground black pepper
½ tsp fine sea salt

1 In a medium bowl, combine all the ingredients with 3 tablespoons water and whisk together until smooth.

2 If not serving immediately, transfer to an airtight container and keep in the fridge for up to 2 weeks.

Makes
about 260g

Prep time:
10 minutes, plus soaking

Ultimate Umami Paste

- 3 dried shiitake mushrooms
- 100ml boiling water
- 2 tbsp olive oil
- 4 tbsp tomato purée
- 2 tbsp red or brown miso paste
- 3 sheets nori seaweed (the kind used for sushi)
- 25g black olives
- 2 tbsp balsamic vinegar
- 2 tbsp red wine (or swap for red wine vinegar)
- 1 tbsp dark soy sauce
- 1 tbsp brown sugar
- 1 tsp fine sea salt

1. Place the shiitake mushrooms in a small bowl and cover with the boiling water. Leave to rehydrate for 10 minutes.
2. Drain the mushrooms over a bowl and place in a blender with 1 tablespoon of the mushroom soaking liquid and all the remaining ingredients.
3. Blend until very smooth, then transfer to a clean jar and seal with the lid. Keep in the fridge for up to 2 weeks.

Makes about 80g	Prep time: 5 minutes	Cooking time: 8 minutes

Magic Roast Chicken Salt

30g nutritional yeast
1 tbsp garlic granules or garlic powder
1½ tbsp onion granules, or onion powder
1½ tsp celery salt
½ tsp ground white pepper
½ tsp sweet paprika
Pinch of cayenne pepper
1 tsp dried parsley
1 tsp dried thyme
½ tsp dried dill
½ tsp dried chives
½ tsp MSG (optional but encouraged)
2 tsp fine sea salt
2 tsp light brown sugar

1 Preheat the oven to 180°C/160°C Fan/Gas Mark 4 and line a baking tray with baking paper.

2 Spread the nutritional yeast on the prepared baking sheet and roast in the preheated oven for 8 minutes. Check the nutritional yeast during cooking to ensure it's not burning.

3 Immediately after removing from the oven, sprinkle the garlic and onion granules over the hot nutritional yeast and leave to cool to room temperature (about 10 minutes).

4 Place all the ingredients (including the roasted nutritional yeast mixture) into a spice grinder or a high-speed blender and process until fine and uniform.

5 Allow to cool fully after grinding, then transfer to a sealed jar. Keep somewhere dry and dark for up to a month, but ideally use within a few days.

Makes
about 300ml

Prep time:
10 minutes

Cooking time:
8 minutes

Crispy Garlic Chilli Oil

225ml vegetable oil
2 shallots, peeled and finely sliced
4 large garlic cloves, finely sliced
50g crushed red chili flakes
1 tsp coarsely ground black pepper
1 tsp fine sea salt
1 tsp caster sugar
½ tsp MSG (optional but highly encouraged!)
2 tsp soy sauce
1 tbsp black vinegar (or substitute with balsamic vinegar)

1 Put the vegetable oil in a medium saucepan (ideally one with a spout, if you have one) and set over medium heat.

2 After a few minutes, test the oil by dropping in a piece of shallot. If it starts to bubble immediately, the oil is ready. Add the remaining shallots and garlic and for 5–8 minutes, stirring occasionally, until they turn golden brown.

3 Meanwhile, place a few sheets of kitchen paper on a large plate to drain the shallots and garlic once fried.

4 In a large heatproof bowl (ideally stainless steel), combine the remaining ingredients.

5 Once the garlic and shallots are golden brown, remove them from the oil with a slotted spoon or spider strainer and transfer them to the prepared plate to drain.

6 Carefully pour the hot oil over the chlili flake mixture in the bowl. The mixture will bubble violently, so be cautious of the steam and use an oven mitt if you have one.

7 Let the mixture cool for 5 minutes, then add the crispy garlic and shallots to the oil.

8 While the mixture is still warm, spoon it into sterilized jars, seal, and store in the fridge for up to 6 months. The flavour will develop over time, so try not to open it for at least a week after making.

Makes
4-6 servings

Prep time:
5 minutes

Cooking time:
10 minutes

Pickled Pink Onions

1 large red onion
60ml white wine vinegar (or any white vinegar, or the juice of 2 lemons)
1 tsp fine sea salt
1 tsp brown sugar

1 Slice the red onion very finely. Use a kitchen mandolin if you have one. Place the sliced onion in a clean glass jar or bowl.

2 In a jug, combine the vinegar, salt and sugar. Stir well until the salt and sugar dissolve completely.

3 Pour the vinegar mixture over the onions, ensuring they are fully submerged. If needed, press the onions down with a spoon.

4 Cover the jar or bowl and leave at room temperature for 20-30 minutes, stirring occasionally, before serving. For best results, refrigerate for at least an hour or store in the fridge for up to 2 weeks.

Makes about 100g

Prep time: 2 minutes

Cheat's Salsa Macha

- 2 tbsp olive oil
- 1 tbsp mild chilli flakes (chipotle or ancho chilli flakes work best)
- 2 garlic cloves, crushed
- 1 tbsp chipotle paste
- 2 tsp light brown sugar
- 1 tsp red wine vinegar
- ½ tsp fine sea salt
- 2 tbsp chunky natural peanut butter (I use Manilife because it's deep roasted and super chunky)

1. Place a small saucepan or small frying pan over medium heat and add the olive oil.
2. When hot, add the chilli flakes and garlic. Fry for a minute or until browned and fragrant but don't let the garlic burn. Remove from the heat and set aside.
3. In a small bowl, combine all the remaining ingredients and mix until smooth and well combined. Add the chilli and garlic oil then mix again. Taste and adjust seasoning as needed, adding more salt or sugar to balance the heat.
4. Store in an airtight container in the fridge for up to 2 weeks.

Index

D

E

F

N

O

P

Acknowledgements

Samhita Foria - I'm so pleased we got to work on this together. Your energy and enthusiasm carried this from dream to reality. You knew what I was trying to do from square one and you have helped me to deliver something I'm really proud of. Thank you!

Richard Pike - Thank you for the support from start to finish. I think you're actually going to get a lot of use out of this one!

Rebecca Woods - From your food styling to your editing, I couldn't have done this without you. You're truly multi-talented and I'm so glad we got to know each other over the shoot (despite the occasional water shut-off and over-stuffed fridge).

Claire Rochford - I have no idea how you immediately got the visual vibe so right for this book, but I'm beyond grateful. You've been so fun and responsive to work with and I can't wait to hold this book in my hands!

Husband and Ripley - What a team we are!? I love you both so much.

BLOOMSBURY PUBLISHING
Bloomsbury Publishing Plc
50 Bedford Square, London, WC1B 3DP, UK
29 Earlsfort Terrace, Dublin 2, Ireland
29 Earlsfort Terrace, Dublin 2, D02 AY28, Ireland

First published in Great Britain 2026

A catalogue record for this book is available from the British Library

ISBN: HB: 978-1-5266-3845-8; ebook: 978-1-5266-3843-4

2 4 6 8 10 9 7 5 3 1

Commissioning Editor: Samhita Foria
Copyeditor: Rebecca Woods
Designer: Claire Rochford
Food Stylist: Rebecca Woods
Production: Laura Brodie

Printed and bound in China by C&C Offset Printing Co., Ltd.

To find out more about our authors and books visit www.bloomsbury.com
and sign up for our newsletters. For product safety related questions contact
productsafety@bloomsbury.com